Common Core
Writing Companion

HIGH SCHOOL—Level A

Perfection Learning®

EDITORIAL DIRECTOR:	CAROL FRANCIS
EXECUTIVE EDITOR:	JIM STRICKLER
EDITOR:	ANDREA STARK
PROOFREADING COORDINATOR:	SHERI COOPER
ART DIRECTION:	RANDY MESSER
DESIGNER:	TOBI CUNNINGHAM
COVER:	MIKE ASPENGREN

REVIEWERS:

MARCIA PUNSALAN
9th Grade Language Arts Teacher
Clay High School
Oregon City Schools
Oregon, Ohio

DEBORA STONICH
Coordinator of Secondary Language Arts and Journalism
McKinney ISD
McKinney, Texas

© 2013 by Perfection Learning®

Please visit our Web site at:
www.perfectionlearning.com

When ordering this book, please specify:
ISBN: 978-0-7891-8457-3 or **99746**

10 11 12 13 PP 20 19 18 17

Table of Contents

Meeting the Common Core State Standards   5

Chapter 1   Characteristics of Good Writing   **6**   CCSS W.9–10.4

   Lesson 1   Development   6
   Lesson 2   Organization   9
   Lesson 3   Evidence   11
   Lesson 4   Language and Style   13
   Lesson 5   Conventions in Writing   14

Chapter 2   Writing an Argumentative Essay   **15**   CCSS W. 9–10.1

   Lesson 1   Claims   15
   Lesson 2   Support for Claims   18
   Lesson 3   Counterclaims   20
   Lesson 4   Evidence from Sources   21
   Lesson 5   How to Write an Argumentative Essay   24
   Lesson 6   You Try It   33

Chapter 3   Writing an Informative Essay   **34**   CCSS W. 9–10.2

   Lesson 1   Thesis Statement   34
   Lesson 2   Support for the Thesis Statement   36
   Lesson 3   Analyzing Sources   37
   Lesson 4   How to Write an Informative Essay   39
   Lesson 5   You Try It   48

Chapter 4   Reporting on Research   **49**   CCSS W. 9–10.7

   Lesson 1   Topics for Research   49
   Lesson 2   Relevant Information   51
   Lesson 3   Synthesis of Sources   55
   Lesson 4   Citations and Quotations   57
   Lesson 5   How to Write a Research Report   59
   Lesson 6   You Try It   69

Chapter 5 Writing a Literary Analysis   **70**   **CCSS W. 9–10.9**

    Lesson 1   Elements of a Literary Analysis   70

    Lesson 2   Evidence from Texts   72

    Lesson 3   How to Write a Literary Analysis   76

    Lesson 4   You Try It   85

Chapter 6   Writing a Narrative   **86**   **CCSS W. 9–10.3**

    Lesson 1   Point of View   86

    Lesson 2   Narrative Techniques   87

    Lesson 3   Sequence of Events   88

    Lesson 4   Descriptive Language   89

    Lesson 5   Conclusion   90

    Lesson 6   How to Write a Narrative   91

    Lesson 7   You Try It   97

Chapter 7   Tips for Success   **98**

    Lesson 1   Ten Tips for Quick Revision   98

    Lesson 2   General Test-Taking Tips   100

    Lesson 3   Tips for Speaking and Listening   102

Meeting the Common Core State Standards

The Common Core State Standards declare the importance of writing to texts—of drawing knowledge from sources and using what you learn to help you express your ideas clearly:

> For students, writing is a key means of asserting and defending claims, showing what they know about a subject, and conveying what they have experienced, imagined, thought, and felt.

The instruction and activities in this book will prepare you to meet the standards. If you do, you will score well on the assessments based on them.

What Are the Characteristics of Good Writing?

Your writing will be evaluated according to how well it shows the basic characteristics found in all types of good writing:

- *Development:* Does the text state the key idea clearly and support it strongly?

- *Organization:* Does the text include an introduction, body, and conclusion? Are transitions from one idea to another smooth and logical?

- *Evidence:* Is the information in the text relevant and strong?

- *Language and Style:* Does the text use words precisely? Is the tone appropriate?

- *Grammar, Spelling, and Punctuation:* Does the text use standard grammar, spelling, and punctuation?

How Is This Book Organized?

The first chapter of this book provides instruction and activities to help develop the characteristics of good writing listed above.

Each of the next five chapters focuses on a different type of writing.

- arguments
- informative/explanatory texts
- research reports
- literary analyses
- narratives

In each of these five chapters, the first several lessons highlight the elements particularly important to one type of writing. For example, the chapter on arguments includes lessons that focus on claims and counterclaims.

The next to last lesson in each chapter takes you, step by step, through writing a text. Built into these lessons are instruction and practice in grammar and usage that address the most common writing problems.

The final lesson in each chapter provides prompts for you to demonstrate your skills in gathering, analyzing, and using information in your writing. This lesson ends with a checklist based on the characteristics of good writing.

Chapter 1

Characteristics of Good Writing

No matter what type of writing you are asked to do, there are some common characteristics that all good writing shares. These are important for you to understand because your writing will be evaluated on these qualities.

Good writing
- is **well developed**
- has a **cohesive organization**
- contains **evidence** from sources to support main points
- uses **precise language** and a formal **style**
- follows rules of **standard grammar, spelling,** and **punctuation**

LESSON 1 DEVELOPMENT

Well-developed writing focuses in on a main idea. This central idea is then expanded with interesting details, relevant facts, or carefully chosen evidence. The writer has a clear purpose that is appropriate to the task and the audience.

Activity 1A Finding the Main Idea

Read the following paragraph and underline the main idea.
Then answer the question that follows.

> In recent years, contemporary music has become more and more international in scope. One noteworthy example is the music associated with cellist Yo-Yo Ma's Silk Road Ensemble. The group, influenced by the flow of ideas along the ancient trade road between Europe and Asia, has selected and performed traditional music from countries such as Turkey, Armenia, and China. Selections are typically performed on Western instruments blended with traditional instruments from the countries where the compositions originated. The resulting music, a mix of old and new, is intended to draw people from diverse cultures together.

1. What is the purpose of the passage?

_____

_____

Purposes for Writing

Common writing purposes include informing, explaining, narrating a real or imagined story, and presenting an argument to convince readers.

2. How do the supporting details develop the main idea?

_____

_____

_____

_____

3. Are the supporting details relevant and sufficient?

_____

_____

_____

_____

> **Relevant and Sufficient**
> ....
> - Relevant details relate to the main idea.
> - Sufficient details mean there are enough details to answer the main questions the reader has about the topic.

 ### Activity 1B *Writing a Paragraph*

Read the following facts about childhood obesity.
Then complete the exercises below.

Health Effects of Childhood Obesity

Childhood obesity has both immediate and long-term effects on health and well-being.

Immediate health effects:

- Obese youth are more likely to have risk factors for cardiovascular disease, such as high cholesterol or high blood pressure.

- In a population-based sample of 5- to 17-year-olds, 70 % of obese youth had at least one risk factor for cardiovascular disease.

- Obese adolescents are more likely to have prediabetes, a condition in which blood glucose levels indicate a high risk for development of diabetes.

- Children and adolescents who are obese are at greater risk for bone and joint problems, sleep apnea, and social and psychological problems such as stigmatization and poor self-esteem.

continued on next page

continued from previous page

Long-term health effects:

- Children and adolescents who are obese are likely to be obese as adults and are therefore more at risk for adult health problems such as heart disease, type 2 diabetes, stroke, several types of cancer, and osteoarthritis.

- One study showed that children who became obese as early as age 2 were more likely to be obese as adults.

- Obesity is associated with increased risk for many types of cancer, including cancer of the breast, colon, endometrium, esophagus, kidney, pancreas, gall bladder, thyroid, ovary, cervix, and prostate, as well as multiple myeloma and Hodgkin's lymphoma.

1. Use the passage as a source of information for a paragraph of your own. Write a main idea statement for your paragraph.

_____

_____

_____

Collaboration on Paragraphs

Use the following questions to evaluate a partner's paragraph: Is the purpose clear? Is the main idea well developed? Are there sufficient supporting details?

2. Go back to the passage and underline four details you can use to support your main idea statement.

3. Write a paragraph for an audience of parents. Be sure your paragraph includes both your main idea statement and good supporting details. Put the information in your own words. Do not merely copy sentences from the passage.

_____

_____

_____

_____

_____

_____

_____

_____

LESSON 2 ORGANIZATION

A well-organized text has a clear beginning, middle, and ending. It presents details in a logical order so that the reader can follow the train of thought. Transitional words and phrases help the reader understand how ideas fit together cohesively, resulting in a piece of writing with unity and clarity.

Organization	Used in	Transitional phrases
Chronological: time order	Narrative writing to explain events Informational/explanatory writing to explain steps in a process	*First, next, later, afterward, a few days later, at the same time*
Order of Importance: least to most important or most to least important	Argumentative writing to explain reasons Informational/explanatory writing to explain details	*First, another reason, however, on the other hand, finally*
Spatial Order: arranged according to location	Informational/explanatory writing to describe places and things	*In the upper corner, across, next to, under, beneath*
Comparison and Contrast: similarities and differences	Informational/explanatory writing to show how things are alike or different	*Similarly, in the same way, on the other hand, but, conversely*

Activity 2A Analyzing a Paragraph

Read the following passage. Then complete the exercises on the following page.

Students should be allowed to bring and use their own iPads, ebook readers, and laptops at school. The main reason this is a good idea is that technology enhances learning. Students would have greater access to information for research projects and would be able to incorporate digital elements into their writing and speaking projects. Studies have shown that students with access to a laptop at school significantly outscore a control group in the areas of mathematics and language arts. Another reason to allow students to bring their own technology is to save the school district money by shifting the burden of providing computers for students from the school to the parents. If a student is unable to afford a laptop, he or she should have priority access to the school's laptops or computers. Students are already using these devices at home. It only makes sense to allow students to enhance their learning by using them at school as well.

1. Underline the main idea of the paragraph.

2. How are the main points organized? Refer to the chart above for organizational structures.

_____

3. Circle transitional words and phrases that help the reader make connections between the ideas.

Activity 2B Writing a Paragraph

You are applying to become a volunteer at a local animal shelter. One of the requirements is that you write a paragraph that explains why you would be a good member of their volunteer staff. Study the following information found on the shelter's Web site. Then write a well-organized paragraph on the lines below. Refer to specific details from the excerpt in your paragraph.

- Volunteers must commit to a regular schedule with a minimum of 2 hours per week of duties.

- Volunteers must be at least 10 years old. Volunteers younger than 16 must be accompanied by a parent or legal guardian.

- Students must be mature, dependable, ambitious, and able to follow instructions and work independently on assigned tasks.

- Students with a negative attitude, careless work ethic, inability to follow instructions, or unreliability will be terminated from the program.

_____

_____

_____

_____

_____

Collaboration on Organization

Use the following questions to evaluate a partner's paragraph:

- Is the organization of the paragraph clear?

- Are appropriate transitional words and phrases used to connect ideas?

- Do the ideas flow in a logical order? Give your partner specific suggestions of how they can improve the organization of his or her paragraph. Revise your paragraphs on the basis of your partner's and your own evaluation.

LESSON 3 EVIDENCE

Often a prompt will ask you to develop your essay by providing textual evidence. **Textual evidence** includes direct quotations and references to specific information found in the reading. Gather evidence by reading texts closely and drawing information from them.

Activity 3A Analyzing a Paragraph

Read the following paragraph. Then complete the exercises below.

> In the book *To Kill a Mockingbird,* the mockingbird is a symbol of innocence. In chapter 10, Scout's father says that it's a sin to kill a mockingbird. Later, Scout's neighbor explains that mockingbirds "don't do one thing but . . . sing their hearts out for us." Throughout the rest of the book, many innocent characters are introduced including Tom Robinson who is falsely accused of raping a white woman and Boo Radley, a mysterious man who never leaves his decrepit house. The killing of Tom Robinson is compared to "the senseless slaughter of songbirds." Scout herself comes to understand that hurting Boo Radley is like shooting a mockingbird. By the end of the book, killing a mockingbird is clearly linked to destroying innocence.

1. Underline three examples of textual evidence.

2. Is there adequate textual evidence to support the main idea? Why or why not?

_____

_____

_____

_____

_____

_____

_____

_____

Activity 3B Writing a Paragraph

Read the following quotations. Then follow the directions below.

> It is not the critic who counts; not the man who points out how the strong man stumbles, or where the doer of deeds could have done them better. The credit belongs to the man who is actually in the arena, whose face is marred by dust and sweat and blood; who strives valiantly; who errs, who comes short again and again, because there is no effort without error and shortcoming; but who does actually strive to do the deeds; who knows great enthusiasms, the great devotions; who spends himself in a worthy cause; who at the best knows in the end the triumph of high achievement, and who at the worst, if he fails, at least fails while daring greatly, so that his place shall never be with those cold and timid souls who neither know victory nor defeat.
>
> —Theodore Roosevelt
>
> Success is not final, failure is not fatal: it is the courage to continue that counts.
>
> —Winston Churchill

Write a paragraph explaining the relationship between courage and failure. Support your ideas using evidence from the passages above.

_____

_____

_____

_____

_____

_____

_____

_____

_____

_____

_____

_____

Collaboration on Evidence

Use the following questions to evaluate a partner's paragraph:

- Does the paragraph use evidence from the text?

- Is the evidence effective?

- Does it reinforce the writer's ideas?

- Give your partner specific details as you answer these questions. Revise your paragraphs on the basis of your partner's and your own evaluation.

LESSON 4 LANGUAGE AND STYLE

Good writing uses **language** that is precise and clear. Words are carefully chosen to help the reader "see" what is being described. Verbs are mostly active voice; nouns are specific, not trite. The **style** of the writing is formal, avoiding slang and personal pronouns.

Activity 4A Analyzing a Paragraph

Read the following paragraph and underline four examples of clear, precise language.

A cool stream trickles along the western slopes of the Great Smoky Mountains. Overhead, in a canopy of trees, red squirrels and martens play. The bucolic scene gives no hint of the invasion being waged by a tiny insect known as the hemlock woolly adelgid. This tiny, aphid-like pest has inflicted massive damage to the hemlock trees in the area. Female adelgids secrete a white, wool-like material on hemlock branches as they lay their eggs. When the eggs hatch, the young feed on the hemlock's sap, which gradually kills the tree over a 4 to 15 year span.

Activity 4B Writing a Paragraph

Choose a topic you have studied recently in a science or history class. Write a paragraph that demonstrates clear, precise language and formal style.

_____

_____

_____

_____

_____

_____

_____

_____

_____

_____

LESSON 5 CONVENTIONS IN WRITING

Using correct **grammar, spelling,** and **punctuation** is the finishing touch on an effective essay. Using verbs incorrectly, misspelling words, and using commas incorrectly can prevent your readers from understanding what you have written. For example, "Let's add basil" could mean to add an herb, basil, to a dish of food. "Let's add Basil" could mean to add a person named Basil to a group.

Activity 5A Editing a Paragraph

Edit the paragraph for mistakes in grammar, spelling, and punctuation by rewriting it correctly on the lines below.

The final reason why the city should not build the bus shelters perposed by the Mayor is that there ugly. I see the material that will be used to construct them, and I'm convinced they looked like World war II bunkers. The advertising posters that will cover the back of each shelter is gaudy and will obstruct vision. The overall affect will be hulking and clumsy, no wonder the merchants hate them! Downtown Lincoln avenue wont be a popular tourist destination no longer if these monstrosities are allowed to be builded.

_____

_____

_____

_____

_____

_____

_____

_____

_____

_____

_____

Collaboration on Editing

Use the following to evaluate a partner's paragraph:

- Are all spelling errors corrected?

- Was a run-on sentence corrected?

- Are verb tenses consistent throughout the paragraph? Identify specific errors that should be corrected. Revise your paragraphs on the basis of your partner's and your own evaluation.

Chapter 2

Writing an Argumentative Essay

How do you get people to agree with you? One way is to present them with an argument and support for it.

LESSON 1 CLAIMS

In an argumentative essay, you begin by making a claim. A **claim** is the main point you want readers to accept. It is more than just an opinion about a personal preference. It is a precise statement that you

- think is true
- can support with accurate and reasonable information
- expect some readers will disagree with

One example of a claim is, "Today's teenagers are more serious about school than teenagers were 30 years ago." Some people, but not all, will agree. Both supporters and opponents of it might back their claims with reasons that explain why one generation of students might work harder than another. Both might cite evidence from surveys showing how student attitudes toward school have changed in the past 30 years.

The claim in an argumentative essay almost always appears in the first paragraph. Often it is the last sentence.

Activity 1A *Identifying Claims*

Imagine your school is debating whether to ban shirts with slogans supporting political candidates. Underline the claim in this paragraph and explain why you selected it.

> The school dress code bans "all clothing that expresses controversial language." Since people disagree on the meaning of controversial, enforcing this code fairly is difficult. A close look at four cases from the past school year shows that, in practice, this ban prohibits most but not all clothing with the names of political candidates. Further, the ban sometimes prohibits and sometimes allows clothing that encourages illegal activities. These cases show that the ban needs to be revised so that it is more precise.

_____

_____

_____

_____

_____

Types of Claims

Most claims serve one of the following purposes:

- clarify a definition
- explain a cause or effect
- make a judgment
- advocate an action

Activity 1B Making Claims Precise

Of the three claims listed, label the one that is most precise as "good."
Revise the other two claims to make them more precise.

Claim	Revision
1. People should encourage students to do their homework because it will help them.	
2. Do some teachers already give extra credit to students for showing school spirit?	
3. High schools should require students to volunteer 20 hours per year in the community.	

Activity 1C Identifying Claims for Argument

In each row below, compare the statements in the first and second columns. Then explain why the statement in the Better Claim column is more effective as a claim for an argumentative essay.

Weak Claim	Better Claim	Explanation
1. *Catcher in the Rye* was written by J. D. Salinger and first published in 1951.	*Catcher in the Rye* describes the difficulties of growing up anywhere, not just in the United States.	
2. Many adults enjoy reading novels.	Reading novels such as *Catcher in the Rye* helps students to develop their imagination.	
3. I liked *Huckleberry Finn* more than *Catcher in the Rye*.	*Huckleberry Finn* tells readers more about American culture than does *Catcher in the Rye*.	

Activity 1D Writing a Claim

Below is an excerpt from a government report on post-high school education. Read the passage and then write a claim that you can support using this passage. An associate's degree is usually earned in two years.

Students Earn More Associate's Degrees and Vocational Certificates; Up 25 Percent in 5 years

Largest jumps for Black and Hispanic women; seen in health care, proprietary schools

The number of associate's degrees and vocational certificates awarded by postsecondary institutions has reached almost 1.5 million, according to a new report from the National Center for Educational Statistics.

Most of this growth was driven by women seeking credentials in health care fields—in particular, Black and Hispanic women. Health care accounted for 31 percent of all certificates and associate degrees awarded in 2007 and increased 68 percent over the decade studied.

The report, "Changes in Postsecondary Awards Below the Bachelor's Degree: 1997-2007," comes at a time when the labor market demand is growing for jobs requiring these types of credentials. Tom Weko, associate commissioner for the postsecondary division at NCES, said the increase is driven by both labor demands and a demographic bubble of people entering college-age years.

Source: United States Department of Education, Institute of Education Sciences.

LESSON 2 SUPPORT FOR CLAIMS

To win your readers to your point of view, you need to support your claim as strongly as you can. Most support is one of two kinds:

- **Evidence** includes facts and informed judgments.
- **Reasons** include logical conclusions from evidence or ideas.

> ### Strength of Support
>
> Support is strong if it comes from a reliable source and is stated precisely. In general, more recent information is stronger than older information.

Activity 2A *Identifying Strong Support*

Each box includes a pair of similar sentences that might be used in an essay about whether the school day should be longer. In each pair, underline the words that differ. In the Explanation box, explain why one sentence provides stronger support for a claim than the other one does.

A. Students learned more after schools lengthened their day, according to a study released in 1989.	B. Students learned more after schools lengthened their day, according to a study released last week.

1. Explanation

C. Since last year, I have strongly believed that if the school day were longer, students would learn more.	D. A study by three researchers found that if the school day were longer, students would learn more.

2. Explanation

E. Many students have probably said, at least once, that they think they would learn more if the school day were longer.	F. In an all-school survey, 72 percent of students said that they think they would learn more if the school day were longer.

3. Explanation

Activity 2B *Identifying Support for Claims*

Read the following passage and follow the directions below it.

Students and Language

The number of school-age children who spoke a language other than English at home rose from 4.7 to 11.2 million between 1980 and 2009, or from 10 to 21 percent of the population in this age range. The percentage of school-age children who spoke a language other than English at home and spoke English with difficulty increased from 4 to 7 percent between 1980 and 2000, and then decreased to 5 percent in 2009.

Source: Adapted from the United States Department of Education, National Center for Educational Statistics.

> ### Multiple Claims
>
> One fact can support alternate or even opposing claims. For example, between 1990 and 2010, the school dropout rate fell from 12 percent to 7 percent. This could support either a claim that schools were improving or a claim that too many students are dropping out.

1. Underline a phrase or sentence in the text that supports this claim:

   "The United States became more ethnically diverse in the late 1900s and early 2000s."

2. Underline a phrase or sentence in the text that supports this claim:

   "Changes in school programs and technology in the early 2000s helped immigrant students learn to speak English."

LESSON 3 COUNTERCLAIMS

In addition to showing evidence that supports your claim, you should present the view of those who disagree with you. A statement that disagrees with your claim is a **counterclaim.** For example, if you claim that your school has the best basketball team in the conference, possible counterclaims include the following:

- Another school's team is the best in the conference.
- Another school's team is better than your school's team.

In an argumentative essay, you should recognize the counterclaims of those who disagree with you and respond to their evidence.

Anticipating Concerns

Anticipate and respond to your audience's concerns that might make them support a counterclaim. If you respond fairly, you will strengthen your argument.

Activity 3A *Writing Counterclaims*

For each claim listed below, write a counterclaim.

Claim	Counterclaim
1. If schools pay students for high grades, students will study harder.	
2. Schools have a right to suspend students who break a law even if they do so off school property.	
3. The right of principals to maintain order should include the right to search student lockers.	

Activity 3B *Responding to Counterclaims*

In the following paragraph, the claim is stated in the first sentence. Underline the counterclaim and the evidence supporting it. Circle the response to the evidence supporting the counterclaim.

If public high schools in the United States required students to wear uniforms, students would learn more. Some people argue that wearing uniforms does not improve student performance. They point out that in Finland, which has one of the best educational systems in the world, students do not wear uniforms. However, evidence from Finland does not apply to the United States because Finnish students are not as diverse as American students.

Words Indicating Counterclaims

You can signal to readers that you are responding to a claim or a counterclaim by starting a sentence with *however, nevertheless, still,* or another adverb that indicates a contrast.

LESSON 4 EVIDENCE FROM SOURCES

Your writing should usually be based on evidence that you get from sources. On some tests, you may be provided with the sources to use. To prepare to use these sources, the test may ask you questions about the source, such as explaining vocabulary used in it, identifying its main idea, and writing a summary of it.

The following set of activities asks questions about a source that provides evidence you could use to write an essay supporting one of two types of school calendars:

- a traditional schedule, with one long summer break

- a year-round schedule, with two-week breaks scattered throughout the year

Activity 4A *Understanding Vocabulary*

Read the following text and answer the vocabulary questions that follow it.

Source 1

Year-Round School Improves Retention
by Mitchell Feldman

The writer is a student at Douglas High School in Parkland, Florida. This article appeared in his school newspaper.

In the early days of the United States educational system, summer vacation was originally created to allow students to work on their family farms during harvest season. Society has changed since then, but our school system has not.

A drastic change is necessary to keep up with the times, and the best option is year-round school.

After spending months outside a learning environment, students forget much of what they learned the previous year.

According to University of Missouri and Tennessee State University, in general, student achievement test scores decline over summer vacation, and summer loss equals about one month on a grade-level equivalent scale. If the vacations were shortened, retention would increase.

Summer vacation also increases the difference between social classes in regards to education. Researchers at John Hopkins University found that "cumulative achievement gains over the first nine years of children's schooling mainly reflect school-year

continued on next page

Types of Sources

Sources can be of several types:

- informational texts, such as news reports and scholarly research
- literary texts, such as novels and poems
- multimedia texts, such as videos

Connecting Sections of Text

In the phrase, "Summer vacation also," the word *also* connects the paragraph with the one before it. Adverbs and adverbial phrases such as *also, furthermore, in addition,* and *more importantly* signal that the writer is presenting additional support for the claim. For more on words that connect paragraphs, see Chapter 6, Writing a Narrative, page 86.

---

continued from previous page

learning, whereas the high [socio-economic status]–low [socio-economic status] achievement gap at ninth grade mainly traces to differential summer learning over the elementary years."

Those of higher income have the ability to access summer schools and tutoring programs, while the lower class does not.

Smaller breaks also allow students to get sufficient sleep. According to researchers at the University of Lübeck, sleep deprivation has a detrimental effect on memory, which was significant after a night of recovery sleep.

With frequent breaks, students have more opportunities to "catch up" on their sleep. The effect is lessened in summer vacation, since sleep has a diminishing effect.

Since the most sleep benefits are obtained in the first part of summer, small breaks would have a greater effect on sleep than one large break. The same diminishing effect holds for the relaxation value of breaks.

Source: *The Courier*, November 10, 2011.

Internet Research

If a source makes references you don't recognize, use a search engine to look them up. For example, if you are not familiar with University of Lübeck, you could quickly find out that it is a famous German university that focuses on medical research.

Part A

Circle the letter before the choice that best explains what the word "retention" means as it is used in this line from the text: "If the vacations were shortened, retention would increase."

- a. absorption
- b. disregard
- c. forgetfulness
- d. maintenance

Part B

Circle the letter before the choice that best helps the reader figure out the meaning of "retention" as used in the text.

- a. "summer loss"
- b. "If the vacations were shortened"
- c. "Summer vacation also increases"
- d. "the difference between social classes"

Vocabulary

A set of "selected response" questions can help you understand what you have just read. Some tests present them in two parts. The first might ask a question about your understanding of the text. The second might ask you to identify the evidence that supports your answer in the first part.

Activity 4B Identifying the Key Idea

Answer the following questions about the key idea of "Year-Round School Improves Retention."

Part A

Circle the letter before the choice that best states Mitchell Feldman's key idea in "Year-Round School Improves Retention."

a. Students need to do agricultural work during vacations.

b. Students should attend school year-round in order to improve their academic performance.

c. Students from wealthier homes benefit more from long vacations than do other students.

d. Students who sleep more will learn more.

Key Idea

The first of a pair of questions might ask you to identify the key idea in a text. A second question might ask you to identify one or more statements that provide evidence for your choice.

Part B

Circle the letters before the two pieces of evidence from "Year-Round School Improves Retention" that support your answer to Part A.

a. "Summer vacation was originally created to allow students to work on their family farms during harvest season."

b. "According to University of Missouri and Tennessee State University, in general, student achievement test scores decline over summer vacation."

c. "the high [socio-economic status]–low [socio-economic status] achievement gap at ninth grade mainly traces to differential summer learning over the elementary years"

d. "sleep deprivation has a detrimental effect on memory, which was significant after a night of recovery sleep"

e. "The effect is lessened in summer vacation, since sleep has a diminishing effect."

Activity 4C Writing a Summary

Write a summary of "Year-Round School Improves Retention."

_____

_____

_____

Collaborating on Summaries

A summary is a shorter version of a text. In a summary, you should include the key idea and the most important support for it. You should leave out most details.

  After you write your summary for this activity, share it with another student through e-mail or a social media site and ask him or her to evaluate it.

LESSON 5

HOW TO WRITE AN ARGUMENTATIVE ESSAY

Below is a second source about the school-year calendar. Following it is a model demonstrating the five steps in writing an argumentative essay. Use these five steps to help you write your own essays.

> ### Source 2
>
> ### Defending the Traditional Schedule, by Boyd F. Jensen
>
> *The Salt Lake City, Utah, school district experimented with year-round schools. Instead of a traditional schedule in which students had one long summer break, students went to school all year and had short breaks throughout it. This text expresses one person's reflections on the success of the experiment. His claim is that year-round school does not increase student achievement.*
>
> Of the district's elementary year-round schools, only half made Adequate Yearly Progress [a measure of academic progress] last year—a federal government requirement. Eighty percent of the traditional calendar elementary schools made Adequate Yearly Progress.
>
> According to the superintendent, it costs $128,000 more just in busing expenses to keep the schools operating under the year-round calendar. If we took this savings from busing, we could offer students more than 20,000 small-group tutoring hours during the school year. Small-group tutoring is a proven way to increase academic performance. Shouldn't we invest in a sure thing rather than continuing to throw good money at a bad program?
>
> Source: *Deseret News*, January 30, 2011.

Using Multiple Sources

When writing an argumentative essay for a test, you might be asked to read additional sources about the same topic as a source you have already read and answered questions about. These additional sources will provide more evidence to use in your essay.

Step 1. Understand the prompt.

The directions for writing an essay are called the **prompt.** The verbs in it tell you what to do. Here is an example of a prompt:

> You have read texts by two writers commenting on year-round schools. Write an essay that defends a claim concerning the school calendar. You might favor the traditional schedule or you might favor year-round schools. Use textual evidence from the sources to support your claim.

Activity 5A Analyzing the Prompt

In the prompt on page 24, underline up to 20 key words that tell you what to do. Then, rewrite the prompt in your own words.

_____

_____

_____

_____

_____

Collaborate About Prompts

....

After you write your prompt, trade it with a partner. Discuss any differences in how you interpreted the prompt.

Step 2. Take notes on the sources.

You may have already analyzed the sources, but now you should take notes on them with the prompt in mind. Look for specific statements that you can use in your essay. If you use a graphic organizer, choose one that fits the directions stated in the prompt. See the table below for some ideas. After taking notes, you should state the claim you want to defend and at least one counterclaim.

Words in the Prompt	Type of Graphic Organizer	Model
compare, contrast, distinguish	Venn diagram	
identify causes, explain effects	flow chart	
summarize, describe	web diagram	
evaluate, judge, weigh	two-column chart	

Activity 5B Analyzing Sources

The chart below includes notes from the two sources about year-round schools shown on previous pages.

1. In the row for Academic Progress, circle the words that indicate whether the information came from the first or the second source.

2. Fill in one of the empty cells in the Cost row.

3. Fill in one of the empty cells in the Achievement Gap row.

4. In the final row of the chart, write a counterclaim.

Issue	Support for Year-Round Schools	Support for the Traditional School-Year
Academic Progress	Researchers at the University of Missouri and Tennessee State University found that, in general, student achievement test scores decline the equal of about one month on a grade-level equivalent scale (Feldman).	In Salt Lake City, students at year-round schools did not make as much progress as students at traditional schools (Jensen).
Cost		
Achievement Gap		
My Claim: Schools should keep the traditional school year.		
A Counterclaim:		

Step 3. Organize your ideas.

Use an outline to organize the ideas for your essay. Like most texts, an argumentative essay should include an introduction, body, and conclusion.

The **introduction** is the first paragraph of an essay. It should identify the topic and state the claim.

The **body** is the main part of an essay. It should present the support for the claim—both reasons and evidence. In addition, it should present at least one counterclaim and a response to it. Below are three options for organizing the body of the essay.

Option	What to Present First	What to Present Second	Strength
Option 1	Support for the claim	Counterclaims and responses to it	Simple organization: support flows smoothly from the statement of the claim in the first paragraph
Option 2	Counterclaims and responses to it	Support for the claim	Often used when the writer expects most readers to initially agree with the counterclaim so that the writer can confront their views immediately
Option 3	Present issue by issue, alternating between support for claims and responding to counterclaims		Excellent for long essays that include many counterclaims

The **conclusion** is the last paragraph of an essay. It should either summarize the main support for the claim or state the strongest support for the claim. It should always restate the claim.

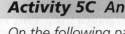

Activity 5C Analyzing an Outline

On the following page is an outline that a student might have written before drafting an argumentative essay about year-round schools. As you read it, mark it as follows:

1. Circle the heading for each of the three main parts of the outline.

2. Underline the two places where the claim is specifically mentioned.

3. Write a note in the margin to identify a counterclaim or evidence supporting it.

4. Write a note in the margin to explain how the first three entries under "II. Body" are similar.

> ### Strong Ending
> Often, the last line of the conclusion is a short or dramatic sentence that will stick in the minds of readers.

Sample Outline: Keeping the Traditional School Calendar

Claim: Schools should keep the traditional school year.

I. Introduction

   A. Summer is the best time of year to be out of school.

   B. Schools should keep the traditional schedule.

II. Body

   A. Traditional schedule saves money. Use evidence about Salt Lake City.

   B. Some research shows that year-round school helps students learn more. Use evidence from Missouri and Tennessee State.

   C. Many students do better with the traditional schedule. Use evidence from Salt Lake City.

   D. Maybe students forget as much during all of the two-week breaks as they do over a summer.

   E. Wealthy students benefit more from summer vacation. Schools should do things to help low-income students.

III. Conclusion

   A. Summarize main evidence.

   B. Repeat claim about keeping the traditional schedule.

Step 4. Write the draft.

Using your notes and your outline, write your essay.

Activity 5D Analyzing Organization

On the next page is the draft of an essay about year-round schools. As you read it, mark it as indicated below. The draft includes some mistakes in punctuation, spelling, grammar, and usage that you will be asked to correct in the next activity.

1. Write a note in the margin to identify the introduction.

2. Underline the claim.

3. Place a check mark in the margin beside three specific pieces of evidence from the sources.

4. Double underline the counterclaim.

5. Circle three words that indicate the writer is responding to a counterclaim.

6. Write a note in the margin to identify the conclusion.

Spell Check

If you write your essay on a computer, spell-check will highlight many errors. However, it may not catch a mistake if the mistake is also a correctly spelled word. Imagine you meant to write "It's over here, then." Instead, you typed "Its over hear, than." Spell-check might miss all three errors in the sentence.

Sample Draft: Keeping the Traditional School Calendar

Most young people in this community consider summer there favorite season. They can enjoy baseball, swimming, and going barefoot. How can anyone imagine spending this wonderful season trapped in a school building. Advocates of changing to year-round school can. However, the evidence does not support their position. Schools should keep the traditional schedule because it is better for all students.

Benefits of Traditional Schedules

The traditional schedule is good for many reasons. Besides letting students spend more time outdoors when the weather is good, it saves money compared to a year-round school. In Salt Lake City, busing costs alone was increased $180,000 when the schools tried a year-round system. Schools can always use more money for new equipment, more activities, or better pay for teachers. Schools should not spend money to make a change, that is not necessarily helpful.

The most important argument in favor of year-round schools is about academics. Some people believe that year-round school will help students learn more if they don't have a long gap in the summer. They point to studies by researchers at the University of Missouri and at Tennessee State. According to this research, students do forget a lot over a long summer break.

However, students also forget over two-week breaks. Evidence suggests that students might forget more in scattered breaks than in one long break. In Salt Lake City, students in year-round schools did not make as much progress as did students at the traditional schools.

The Achievement Gap

People who want year-round schools also say that it gives wealthy students an advantage over poor student. Researchers at Johns Hopkins found that the "achievement gap at ninth grade mainly traces to differential summer learning over the elementary years." However, schools have many ways to address the gap between wealthy and poor students. For examples, schools

Formal Style

Arguments written for tests should have a formal style. This writer sets a formal style in the first sentence. In more informal language, the first sentence could read, "Most kids around here think summer's pretty great."

Citations

In some writing assignments, you will need to identify your sources in your text. For examples showing how to do this, see Chapter 4, Lesson 4, "Citations and Quotations," pages 57–58.

Headings

Adding heads such as "The Achievement Gap" helps the reader see the organization of the essay.

continued on next page

continued from previous page

could apply for money from foundations to provide great, free summer programs that are available for everyone. This would help students of all income levels, but it would be most useful for students whose families cannot afford trips overseas or other special learning opportunities. Changing the school calendar is not necessary to help students learn more during their summer breaks.

Everyone benefits when students learn more. Until researchers produce clear evidence that year-round schools achieve this goal, schools should keep the traditional schedule.

Step 5. Revise your essay.

After you write a draft, read it again carefully. Make any changes you can to improve it. For example, you might rearrange ideas so they flow more smoothly or revise sentences to make them clearer.

In argumentative essays, pay special attention to how you use reasons and evidence based on facts and informed judgments. To make your argument as strong as possible, you should usually present your arguments using the third-person viewpoint, objectively stating what you or other people believe. This means you should

- not use first-person pronouns, such as *I, me, we,* or *our*

- not use second-person pronouns, such as *you.*

> **Issues to Check**
> ....
>
> As you write essays for class assignments, keep a list of specific issues that give you difficulty. Check these issues when you edit your essay.

Activity 5E Maintaining Point of View

The following paragraph is adapted from the student model. Underline the two sentences where the writer switches viewpoints. Then rewrite the sentences to make them consistent with the rest of the paragraph.

People who want year-round schools also say that it gives wealthy students an advantage over poor student. Researchers at Johns Hopkins found that the "achievement gap at ninth grade mainly traces to differential summer learning over the elementary years." This makes sense to me. I know I learned a lot about geography, history and the environment on travels with my family on summer vacations.

©Perfection Learning® • No Reproduction Permitted.

On the lines below, rewrite the two sentences that you underlined so they match the viewpoint of the rest of the paragraph.

_____

_____

_____

_____

Step 6. Edit and proofread your essay.

You should follow norms and conventions regarding spelling, punctuation, grammar, and usage. Fix any errors you find and consider changes to make your text flow more smoothly. For example, using colons properly can make your text clearer. One use of colons is with lists. Consider this sentence from the model:

Schools can always use more money for new equipment, more activities, or better pay for teachers.

One way to highlight a list of items and make them stand out from the rest of the sentence is to introduce them with a colon. Following are two options for using a list with a colon.

Option 1

Schools can always use more money for the following: new equipment, after-school activities, and better pay for teachers.

Option 2

Schools can always use more money for the following:

- new equipment
- after-school activities
- better pay for teachers

A colon is often used when a list comes after the phrase *the following*. It is never used after verbs *(is, are, was)* or prepositions *(of, to)*.

You can also use colons to introduce long formal quotations.

In his essay on year-round school, Mitchell Feldman stated his support for this type of schedule: "According to University of Missouri and Tennessee State University, in general, student achievement test scores decline over summer vacation, and summer loss equals about one month on a grade-level equivalent scale. If the vacations were shortened, retention would increase."

Other Uses of Colons

Colons are also used between the chapter and verse in references to the Bible. Example: The minister spoke about Matthew 7:12.

Colons are also used between hours and minutes. Example: The train arrived at 9:15 AM.

Activity 5F Using Colons Effectively

Rewrite each sentence using a colon.

1. They can enjoy baseball, swimming, and going barefoot.

_____

_____

2. Researchers at Johns Hopkins found that the "cumulative achievement gains over the first nine years of children's schooling mainly reflect school-year learning, whereas the high-low achievement gap at ninth grade mainly traces to differential summer learning over the elementary years."

_____

_____

_____

_____

_____

_____

_____

Colons and Semicolons

In a list, the words before the colon may or may not be a sentence. The words in the list after the colon are almost never a sentence. In contrast, a semicolon usually connects two ideas that could each be sentences on their own.

Collaboration on a Thesis Statement

Ask a partner to read your thesis statement. Your partner should tell you whether it is clear and precise, fulfills the requirements of the test prompt, and is based on the texts.

LESSON 6 YOU TRY IT

Now it is your turn to write an argumentative essay. Use what you have learned in this chapter about claims, counterclaims, and evidence. Follow the steps outlined in the last lesson. They are also listed in the box on the right.

Steps in Writing an Argumentative Essay

1. Understand the prompt.
2. Take notes on the sources.
3. Organize your ideas.
4. Write the draft.
5. Revise your essay.
6. Edit and proofread your essay.

Activity 6A *Writing an Argumentative Essay*

Write an argumentative essay in response to one of the following prompts. Use information from at least three sources.

A. Driver's License Age	B. Space Exploration
Most states allow teenagers to get a driver's license at the age of 16. Some people think that young people should not be allowed to drive without supervision until they are 18. Conduct research on the issue and then state a position on whether the driver's license age in your state should be raised to 18. Write an argumentative essay in support of your claim. Address at least one counterclaim and support your ideas with relevant evidence from your research.	In 1961, President John Kennedy set a clear goal for the United States space program: land an astronaut on the moon by the end of the decade. The country succeeded. Conduct research on space exploration today. Then write an argumentative essay stating a claim about space exploration and support it with reasons and evidence. Address at least one counterclaim in your essay.

Checklist

Use the following checklist to edit and revise your essay.

	My writing has . . .
DEVELOPMENT	❒ a clear central claim ❒ strong supporting evidence ❒ one or more counterclaims
ORGANIZATION	❒ a clear introduction, body, and conclusion ❒ good transitions ❒ logical order
EVIDENCE	❒ strong, relevant textual evidence ❒ enough evidence to be convincing
LANGUAGE & STYLE	❒ precise, appropriate word choice ❒ a formal, objective tone
GRAMMAR, SPELLING, & PUNCTUATION	❒ standard grammar ❒ correct spelling ❒ proper punctuation

Writing an Informative Essay

The purpose of an informative/explanatory essay is to explain or to provide information about a topic. When you explain how a bill becomes a law, describe the steps you used in a science experiment, or analyze three causes of the Civil War, you are using informative writing.

LESSON 1 THESIS STATEMENT

The purpose of your informative essay should be communicated in the main idea statement, also called the thesis statement. A **thesis statement** should clearly state the central idea of an essay. It should

- be clear and precise
- fulfill the requirements of the test prompt
- be based upon the texts you were asked to read

A good thesis statement should not begin with "My main idea is . . ." or "In this essay I will. . . ."

> ### Informative Essays
> • Increase the reader's knowledge of a subject
> • Help the reader understand a process or procedure

Activity 1A Making a Thesis Statement Precise

Select the statement below that is most precise and label it "good."
Rewrite the other two to make them more precise.

Thesis Statement	Revision
1. The thing is that there are some steps in the process of becoming a citizen of the United States.	
2. Pets are good for older people.	
3. In his Farewell Address, President Washington warned against the political party system.	

Activity 1B Writing a Thesis Statement

Below is an excerpt from a government report on indicators of climate change. Read the facts and then write a strong thesis statement.

Temperature

- Earth's average temperature has risen by 1.4 degrees F over the past century and is projected to rise another 2.0 to 11.5 degrees F over the next hundred years.

Weather

- More precipitation than 100 years ago; 6 percent more in the United States
- Since the 1980s, hurricanes have gotten stronger as the ocean temperature rises
- More extreme droughts and flooding

Oceans

- Temperatures rising at a rate of 0.2 per decade
- Are becoming more acidic
- Water levels have risen nearly 7 inches in the past 100 years

Source: Environmental Protection Agency.

Thesis Statement:

_____

_____

_____

_____

LESSON 2 SUPPORT FOR THE THESIS STATEMENT

Your thesis statement should be supported with appropriate supporting details. These might include facts, examples, incidents, analogies, or causes and effects. Strong supporting details are relevant, or directly related, to the thesis statement.

Activity 2A Evaluating Supporting Details

Cross out sentences that would not convey good supporting details for the thesis statement. In the margin, write notes explaining why.

> **Thesis Statement: Many students are unhappy about the new federal guidelines for school lunches.**
>
> **Possible Supporting Details**
>
> - Under the new guidelines, lunches for high school students cannot exceed 850 calories.
> - Student athletes are complaining that they don't have enough energy for after-school practices.
> - Most schools charge between $2 and $3 for lunch.
> - New guidelines require schools to offer entrees with less sodium, more whole grains, and a wider selection of fruits and vegetables.
> - At one high school in Wisconsin, the football team led a boycott of the new mandates by refusing to buy lunch.
> - Many students simply dump their vegetables in the garbage.
> - One slice of pepperoni pizza from a local pizzeria contains 300 calories.
> - I believe that the government is taking away students' freedom by controlling what they can and cannot eat.

Activity 2B Writing Supporting Details

Write three good supporting details you might use to support this thesis statement: High school differs from junior high in important ways.

1. _____

_____

2. _____

_____

3. _____

_____

LESSON 3 ANALYZING SOURCES

A test that asks you to write an informative essay may first ask you to read and answer questions about a passage or passages that you will use in writing your essay. If you are asked to write a summary of a text, you should include the main idea and a few key supporting points.

Activity 3A Writing a Summary

Read the following text and write a summary of it on the lines provided.

> ### Source 1
>
> ### Capillary Action
>
> Even if you've never heard of capillary action, it is still important in your life. Capillary action is important for moving water (and all of the things that are dissolved in water). It is defined as the movement of water within the spaces of a porous material due to the forces of adhesion, cohesion, and surface tension.
>
> Capillary action occurs because water is sticky, thanks to the forces of cohesion (water molecules like to stay close together) and adhesion (water molecules are attracted and stick to other substances). Adhesion of water to the walls of a vessel will cause an upward force on the liquid at the edges and result in a meniscus, which turns upward. The surface tension acts to hold the surface intact. Capillary action occurs when the adhesion to the walls is stronger than the cohesive forces between the liquid molecules. The height to which capillary action will take water in a uniform circular tube is limited by surface tension and, of course, gravity.
>
> Not only does water tend to stick together in a drop, it sticks to glass, cloth, organic tissues, soil, and, luckily, to the fibers in a paper towel. Dip a paper towel into a glass of water and the water will "climb" onto the paper towel. In fact, it will keep going up the towel until the pull of gravity is too much for it to overcome.
>
> Source: United States Geological Service.

Types of Sources

Sources can be of several types:

- informational texts, such as report excerpts
- literary texts, such as excerpts from novels
- multimedia texts, such as excerpts from videos
- graphs and charts

Activity 3B Answering Questions About a Source

Read the following text and answer the questions that follow.

Source 2

Capillary action is very useful when cleaning up a mess. When you spill your glass of BubblyBerryPowerGo (which is, of course, mostly water) on the kitchen table, you rush to get a paper towel to wipe it up. First, you can thank surface tension, which keeps the liquid in a nice puddle on the table, instead of a thin film of sugary goo that spreads out onto the floor. When you put the paper towel onto your mess, the liquid adheres itself to the paper fibers and the liquid moves to the spaces between and inside of the fibers.

Plants and trees couldn't thrive without capillary action. Plants put down roots that are capable of carrying water from the soil up into the plant. Water, which contains dissolved nutrients, gets inside the roots and starts climbing up the plant tissue. As water molecule #1 starts climbing, it pulls along water molecule #2, which, of course, is dragging water molecule #3, and so on.

Capillary action is also essential for the drainage of tears from the eye. The tear ducts are constantly producing liquid to keep the eyes moist. Two tiny-diameter tubes, the lacrimal ducts, are present in the inner corner of the eyelid; these ducts secrete tears into the eye.

Source: United States Geological Service.

Part A

Which of the following sentences best summarizes the main idea of the passage?

a. Paper towels rely on capillary action to work.

b. All living things rely on capillary action in some way.

c. Surface tension is important to capillary action.

d. Examples of capillary action are prevalent in the world.

Choose two of the following sentences that could be used to support your answer to Part A.

a. When you spill your glass of BubblyBerryPowerGo (which is, of course, mostly water) on the kitchen table, you rush to get a paper towel to wipe it up.

b. Plants and trees couldn't thrive without capillary action.

c. Capillary action is also essential for the drainage of tears from the eye.

d. The tear ducts are constantly producing liquid to keep the eyes moist.

LESSON 4 HOW TO WRITE AN INFORMATIVE ESSAY

Following is a model demonstrating the steps in writing an informative essay. Use them to help you write your own essays.

Step 1. Understand the prompt.

The directions for writing an essay are called the **prompt.** The verbs in the prompt tell you what to do. Here is an example of a prompt:

> A florist places a white carnation in a glass of water. He adds some blue food coloring to the water. A few days later, the petals of the carnation are tinged with blue. Based upon the texts you read, write an essay explaining the science of capillary action and how it affected what happened to the flower. Be sure to support your ideas with evidence from the text.

Activity 4A Analyzing the Prompt

In the prompt above, underline key words that tell you what to do. Write a purpose statement for your essay below.

My purpose is to: _____

_____

Step 2. Take notes on the sources.

You have already analyzed the sources, but now you should take notes on them with the prompt in mind. Go back to the texts you read. Look for specific statements that will fit with the purpose of your essay.

Activity 4B Gathering Ideas

On the lines below, write some key ideas you will want to include in your essay.

_____

_____

_____

_____

_____

_____

_____

Step 3. Write a thesis statement

Once you've gathered some ideas that you want to include in your essay, you can write a thesis statement. Your thesis statement will be included in the introduction of your essay and will guide the ideas you include in the body of your paper.

Activity 4C Writing a Thesis Statement

Based upon your notes, write a thesis statement for your paper.

_____

_____

_____

_____

Step 4. Organize your ideas.

The next step is to figure out the best order in which to present your ideas. The order should be logical so that the reader can easily follow your train of thought.

You can use a graphic organizer or an outline to organize your ideas. If you use a graphic organizer to organize your main points, choose one that fits the directions stated in the prompt.

Words in the Prompt	Type of Graphic Organizer	Model
compare or contrast	Venn diagram	
cause or effect steps in a process	flow chart	
summarize	web diagram	

Activity 4D Creating a Graphic Organizer

Fill in the flowchart with information from your notes. First, write your thesis statement on the lines. Then fill in details you want to include in your essay.

Thesis Statement

_____

_____

_____

Step 5. Develop a complete outline.

An informative essay should include an introduction, a body, and a conclusion.

The **introduction** should introduce the topic and include the thesis statement.

The **body** should develop the thesis statement using supporting details.

The **conclusion** should restate the thesis statement. It should give a sense of closure to the writing.

> **Defining Terms**
>
> When writing an informative essay on a topic related to science or other technical subjects, explaining unfamiliar vocabulary will help make a complex subject more manageable for both the writer and the reader.

Activity 4E Analyzing an Outline

Below is an outline that a student might have written before drafting an informative essay about capillary action. As you read it, mark it as follows:

1. Circle the heading for each of the three main parts of the outline.

2. Underline the two places where the thesis statement is specifically mentioned.

3. Write the answers to these questions in the margin of the outline: Why is the first paragraph of the body important?

4. Are the main points in the body in logical order? Why or why not?

Sample Outline: The Science of Capillary Action

I. Introduction
   A. A florist places a white flower in a vase of water and blue food coloring. A few days later the flower petals turn blue.
   B. Thesis Statement: Capillary action causes water to flow from the stem to the petals of a plant.

II. Body
   A. Capillary action is the movement of water due to the forces of cohesion, adhesion, and surface tension.

   B. Plants rely on capillary action to grow.
   C. This same phenomenon is demonstrated by the carnation placed in the blue water.

continued on next page

continued from previous page

III. Conclusion

    A. The carnation experiment is just one example of how capillary action works in the world.

    B. From cleaning up a mess with a paper towel to the ducts that secrete tears into the human eye, capillary action is a necessary part of everyday life.

Step 6. Write the draft.

Using your notes and your outline, write your essay.

Activity 4F Analyzing a Draft

Below is the draft of an essay based on the prompt given. As you read it, mark it as follows.

1. Write a note in the margin to identify the introduction and the conclusion.

2. Underline the thesis statement.

3. Place a check in the margin beside three specific pieces of evidence from the sources.

4. Circle three transitional phrases.

> **Style and Tone**
>
> Writing assessments require a formal style. Avoid informal personal pronouns *(I, you)* and slang. Keep the tone objective; avoid giving your personal opinions.

Sample Draft: The Science of Capillary Action

    A florist places a white flower in a vase of water and blue food coloring. A few days later the flowers petals turn blue. What happened? It isn't magic it's science. The science of capillary action explains how the blue water flows from the vase, through the stem, and up to the petals of a plant.

Explanation of Capillary Action

    Capillary action is the movement of water due to the forces of cohesion, adhesion, and surface tension. Cohesion means that water molecules stick together. However, water also likes to stick to other things. This

continued on next page

     Chapter 3 • Writing an Informative Essay **43**

continued from previous page

tendancy is called adhesion. Surface tension holds the surface of the water together so it doesn't run out everywhere. When the force of the water molecule's adhesion to the sides of an object (like a straw) are greater than the cohesion between its molecules, the water will move up the walls of the straw. The water will continue to raise until another force, gravity, stops it.

Capillary Action in Plants

Plants rely on capillary action to grow. A plant puts down roots deep into the soil. Roots absorb the water. Water molecules stick together. Water molecules also stick to the sides of the roots. The water slowly climbs up the roots to the stems. Finally, it arrives at the leaves.

Capillary Action in the Carnation Experiment

This same phenomenon is demonstrated by the carnation placed in the blue water. Capillary action pulls the water up the stem of plant until it reaches the petals. The blue color in the flower pedals clearly demonstrates that the water made it all the way up the stem to the flower.

The carnation experiment is just one example of how capillary action works in the world. There are so many other examples.

Use of Headers

Notice that headers are used to introduce the content of each paragraph in the body. Headers can aid the reader's comprehension, especially when you are writing about complex ideas.

Citations

In some writing assignments, you will need to identify your sources in your text. For examples showing how to do this, see Chapter 4, Lesson 4, "Citations and Quotations," pages 57–58.

Step 7. Revise your essay.

After you write a draft, read it again, watching for problems such as a lack of unity, wordiness, or choppiness. Consider how you would revise the following paragraph about capillary action from the student model.

Plants rely on capillary action to grow. A plant puts down roots deep into the soil. Roots absorb the water. Water molecules stick together. Water molecules also stick to the sides of the roots. The water slowly climbs up the roots to the stems. Finally, it arrives at the leaves.

Notice the length of sentences in this paragraph. They are all short, which makes the writing feel choppy and awkward. Also notice the sentence structure. Nearly all follow the same, simple pattern. Readers will find the overuse of this pattern dull.

One quality of good writing is *fluency*. Fluent writing flows smoothly. When a well-written paragraph is read aloud, it sounds like a musical composition. Too many short, simple sentences cut off the natural rhythm of the words. Solve fluency problems by using a variety of sentence lengths, types, and beginnings.

Analyze the paragraph above for fluency. Notice how the sentence length and structure make the writing engaging and fresh.

- The paragraph opens with two short sentences.
- The third sentence is longer than the first two and begins with a subordinate clause, "When a well-written paragraph is read aloud."
- The fourth sentence contains several describing words before the subject, "Too many short, simple."
- The last sentence includes a list, "lengths, types, and beginnings."

Activity 4G Improving Fluency with Sentence Variety

On the lines below, rewrite the paragraph about capillary action from the student model. Use a variety of sentence lengths and types to make the writing more interesting.

Variety in Sentence Structure

To help you vary your sentence structure, focus on how you start sentences. If you usually begin with the subject, try opening with an adverb or abverbial phrase that modifies the verb in the sentence, such as *Happily* or *During science class*.

_____

_____

_____

_____

_____

_____

_____

_____

_____

_____

_____

_____

_____

_____

Activity 4H Rereading an Essay

Read the draft and answer these questions about possible revisions:

1. Is the thesis statement clear and precise? Explain your answer.

_____

_____

2. Is the thesis statement supported with well-chosen facts? Are the facts sufficient? Are the terms explained clearly?

_____

_____

3. Do words, phrases, and clauses link major sections of the text? Provide two examples to indicate how well the major sections are linked together. Suggest at least one place where transitional phrases could make the writing more cohesive.

_____

_____

4. Does the writing express a formal style and objective tone? Give examples to show whether the text is formal and objective.

_____

_____

5. Is the conclusion of the essay well developed? Rewrite the final paragraph so that the conclusion is stronger.

_____

_____

_____

_____

_____

_____

> **Collaborate on Rereading Essays**
>
> In a small group, discuss the strengths and weaknesses of the draft essay. For example, identify where the draft uses relevant facts, concrete details, and precise language. Also identify where the draft needs revision.

Step 8. Edit and proofread your essay.

After you finish revising the content and style of your essay, read through it carefully to catch and correct any mistakes in grammar, spelling, and punctuation. If you are handwriting your essay, make the corrections neatly and clearly.

As you read over your essay, note any sentences that are not well written. Each sentence should start with a capital letter and end with a period, question mark, or exclamation point.

The following sentence from the model has another type of problem. Can you name it?

It isn't magic it's science.

This is a run-on sentence. A **run-on sentence** is two or more sentences written together as one sentence. Run-ons can be corrected by

- creating two separate sentences
- using the words *and, but, or,* or another conjunction and a comma
- using a semicolon

Activity 4I Correcting Run-on Sentences

Using three different types of correction, rewrite the sentence "It isn't magic it's science." Then place a star by the one you think works best.

1. Two separate sentences

_____

2. One compound sentence with a conjunction *(and, but,* or *or)* that fits the relationship between the two independent clauses

_____

3. One compound sentence joined by a semicolon

_____

Activity 4J Proofreading a Model Essay

Proofread the model essay by finding and correcting the following errors.

1. Two misspelled words

2. An incorrectly used verb

3. A verb that does not agree with its subject

4. A possessive noun without an apostrophe

> ### Pauses and Run-on Sentences
>
> Reading a text aloud can help you identify run-on sentences. Since people naturally pause at the end of each sentence when they talk, listen for the pauses. However, when people are too excited to take a breath, they sometimes speak in run-on sentences.

LESSON 5 YOU TRY IT

 ### Activity 5A *Writing an Informative Essay*

Choose one of the following prompts and write an essay using the steps outlined in this chapter. Then use the checklist to make sure your writing conforms to the Characteristics of Good Writing.

A. Renewable Energy	B. Impact of Internet Access
Using the U.S. Department of Energy Web sites (www.eia.gov and www.energy.gov), conduct research on forms of renewable energy. Then write an informative essay briefly explaining the use of three types of renewable energy. Refer to specific evidence in your essay.	Through computers and smart phones, the Internet provides access to vast stores of information and to people all over the world. Research how extensive Internet access has both positively and negatively affected American life. Write an informative essay that includes specific evidence from your research.

Checklist

Use the following checklist to edit your essay.

My writing has . . .	
DEVELOPMENT	❏ a clear thesis statement ❏ strong supporting points ❏ relevant information based upon research
ORGANIZATION	❏ a clear introduction, body, and conclusion ❏ good transitions ❏ a logical order
EVIDENCE	❏ strong, relevant textual evidence ❏ direct quotations or paraphrased information from other texts
LANGUAGE & STYLE	❏ precise, appropriate word choice ❏ a formal, objective tone
GRAMMAR, SPELLING, & PUNCTUATION	❏ standard grammar ❏ correct spelling ❏ proper punctuation

Steps for Writing an Informative Essay

1. Understand the prompt.
2. Take notes on the sources.
3. Write a thesis statement.
4. Organize your ideas.
5. Develop a complete outline.
6. Write the draft.
7. Revise your essay.
8. Edit and proofread your essay.

Chapter 4

Reporting on Research

In a research report, you gather information from multiple sources to help you answer a question or solve a problem. This process of combining information from different sources into one report is called **synthesizing.**

LESSON 1 TOPICS FOR RESEARCH

The question or problem you research might be identified for you by your teacher or on a test. Or, you may be given a general subject and asked to generate the specific topic yourself. A good topic is

- broad enough that you can easily find multiple sources about it

- narrow enough that you can cover it in the time you have available to research and write

- phrased fairly so that it does not show a strong bias

Following are sample topics for a five-page research report:

Questions to Answer	Problems to Solve
How has Shakespeare's popularity changed over the past four centuries?	Shortage of jobs for high school students during the summer
How useful are algebra and geometry for people after they leave school?	Increase in asthma around the world since the 1980s

Activity 1A Phrasing a Research Question

Select the question that is phrased best for a research project. Then explain your choice.

A. Why are school dropouts so lazy?

B. How many people dropped out of high school last year?

C. Why do students drop out of school?

_____

_____

_____

_____

> ### Fairness in Phrasing
>
> A good question for research allows for more than one reasonable answer. "Why is math a waste of time?" is not a good question because it indicates that the writer already has a strong bias about the topic.

Activity 1B Selecting a Question or Problem

Below are some general subjects for a five-page research report. Underneath each are three possible questions or problems to address in the report. Place a check in the column to indicate which of the three is too broad, which is right in scope, and which is too narrow.

Question or Problem	Too Broad	Right Scope	Too Narrow
1. General Subject: Questions about Voting			
A. How have voting laws and customs changed throughout United States history?			
B. Should the voting age be lowered from 18 to 16?			
C. What is the deadline for registering to vote in the next election?			
2. General Subject: Questions about College Admissions			
A. Are my grades high enough to get into a state university in my state today?			
B. Are students better prepared for college today than they were 30 years ago?			
C. What different guidelines do colleges in the United States today use to decide which applicants to admit?			
3. General Subject: The Problem of Bullying			
A. How my school can reduce bullying			
B. How students all over the world respond to bullies			
C. How I responded to being bullied when I was age 10			

Discuss with a Partner

Talking with a classmate about possible research topics can help you decide whether you need to narrow or broaden the focus of your report.

LESSON 2 RELEVANT INFORMATION

Sources come in many forms. They can be literary or informational, print or digital, words or images. Your report should be based on relevant and authoritative sources:

- **Relevant sources** are ones that include information that is useful for your report.
- **Authoritative sources** are ones produced by knowledgeable individuals that people trust.

Take notes from your sources so that you can remember the information accurately and where you found it. For a classroom assignment, you might want to use notecards. For a test, you might be able to write on the sources that are provided to you.

Activity 2A Identifying Relevant Sources

In the row under each category, circle the title of the source you think would be more useful for a research report on efforts to stop students from smoking. In the space at the end of each row, write a phrase that explains the advantage of the option you circled.

Source 1	Source 2	Explanation
1. Encyclopedia articles		
"Smoking"	"Smoke"	
2. Web sites		
a site advertising low-cost cigarettes	a government-run site with research on why people smoke	
3. Books		
The Easy Way to Stop Smoking, a nonfiction book by Allen Carr	*Smokin' Seventeen*, a novel by Janet Evanovich	
4. News articles		
"When Dying Was Hip: Smoking in the Movies of the 1950s"	"Smoking Trends Between 2002 and 2012"	

Searches for Sources

Learn to use advanced searches to make your research more effective.

- Use words such as *not* and *or* to make your searches broader or narrower. Ask a librarian if you need help.
- Use search terms such as *debate* and *controversy* along with your topic to help you find sources that provide various points of view about a topic.

Reliable Sources

An authority on a topic usually has:

- studied the topic for many years
- no personal interest in selling you a product or idea
- knowledge of current trends, particularly in fast-changing fields such as medical research

Activity 2B Evaluating Reliability

Rate the reliability of each person on the subject of the health effects of smoking. Use a scale of 1, not reliable, to 5, very reliable. Then review your answers and write a description of what makes a source reliable.

_____ A. A doctor who treats lung cancer patients

_____ B. A tobacco company representative

_____ C. A researcher who studies addiction

_____ D. A blogger who writes mostly about music and cars

_____ E. An employee of the state health department

_____ F. A classmate who wrote a research report about smoking

_____ G. An uncle who stopped smoking last year

_____ H. A neighbor who is in sixth grade

> **Collaborate to Evaluate Reliability**
>
> How reliable a person considers a source about a controversial topic might reflect on that person's point of view. If you are uncertain whether to use a source, discuss it with people who do not share your viewpoint.

What makes a source reliable?

_____

_____

_____

Activity 2C Interpreting Sources

Read the following excerpt and answer the questions that follow it.

Of every three young smokers, only one will quit, and one of those remaining smokers will die from tobacco-related causes. Most of these young people never considered the long-term health consequences associated with tobacco use when they started smoking; and nicotine, a highly addictive drug, causes many to continue smoking well into adulthood, often with deadly consequences. . . .

This report examines the social, environmental, advertising, and marketing influences that encourage youth and young adults to initiate and sustain tobacco use. Tobacco products are among the most heavily marketed consumer goods in the U.S. Much of the nearly $10 billion spent on marketing cigarettes each year goes to programs that reduce prices and make cigarettes more affordable; smokeless tobacco products are similarly promoted. Peer influences; imagery and messages that

continued on next page

portray tobacco use as a desirable activity; and environmental cues, including those in both traditional and emerging media platforms, all encourage young people to use tobacco. These influences help attract youth to tobacco use and reinforce the perception that smoking and various forms of tobacco use are a social norm—a particularly strong message during adolescence and young adulthood.

Source: Benjamin, Regina. "Preface." Preventing Tobacco Use Among Youth and Young Adults. Office of the Surgeon General. 2012.

Part A

Circle the letter before the sentence that best expresses the writer's key ideas about smoking.

a. One out of every three young people who start smoking will quit.

b. Young people become addicted to smoking before they understand its risks.

c. Some people consider smoking and other forms of tobacco use a social norm.

d. Smoking is encouraged in both traditional and emerging media platforms.

Part B

Circle the letter before the two statements that provide the most direct evidence for the writer's key idea about smoking.

a. "never considered the long-term health consequences"

b. "this report examines the social, environmental, advertising, and marketing influences"

c. "smokeless tobacco products are similarly promoted"

d. "these influences help attract youth to tobacco use"

> **Two-Part Questions**
>
> Tests may include questions about vocabulary or key ideas followed by a question that asks you to identify the evidence for the answer you provided. These questions may be labeled Part A and Part B.

Activity 2D Taking Notes

Write three phrases or sentences from the source in the previous activity that you think would be useful in a research report about tobacco use among students. Explain why you choose these phrases or sentences.

_____

_____

_____

_____

_____

_____

Activity 2E Comparing Notes

Below are examples of two notes based on the same source. Explain which note is more useful.

> The 1964 report on the health hazards of smoking marked the beginning of a series of authoritative scientific statements by the Surgeon General. These reports have commanded public attention and have helped shape the debate on the responsibility of government, physicians, and individual citizens for the nation's health.

A. A 1964 report on smoking was the first of several "authoritative scientific statements" by the Surgeon General

B. The Surgeon General has issued many important reports.

_____

_____

_____

_____

Practice Taking Notes

To take notes successfully, you need to pick up the important information. You can practice the skill of identifying important information every time you read. For example, when you read a story about a football game or a review of a movie, select the most important statements.

LESSON 3 SYNTHESIS OF SOURCES

Research includes finding multiple sources of information and integrating that information into one report. This process of combining parts into a new whole is called synthesizing. One challenge when **synthesizing** is to maintain the flow of ideas.

- Connect an idea that builds on the one already stated using words and phrases such as *in addition, consequently,* and *as a result.*

- Contrast an idea with one already stated using words and phrases such as *however, consequently,* and *in contrast.*

Activity 3A Identifying the Flow of Ideas

In the following passage, circle four words or phrases at the beginnings of sentences that help one idea flow into another.

Geography classes are increasingly important. More and more students will travel abroad during their lifetimes. All of this travel means that students will have more contact with people from other countries. Students should know about the lands they might visit. In addition, more and more students will work with, or for, foreign companies. Students need to understand the business customs of other countries. However, geography should not dwell on little facts. Rather than memorizing country capitals, students should learn how the features of a region influence the inhabitants.

Activity 3B Connecting Related Ideas

Write a paragraph that synthesizes these two comments. Poet Robert Frost said, "I am not a teacher, but an awakener." Historian Plutarch said, "The mind is not a vessel to be filled, but a fire to be kindled."

_____

_____

_____

_____

_____

_____

_____

Trade Paragraphs

After completing Connecting Related Ideas, exchange your paragraph with a classmate. Read each other's answer aloud. Listen as you read for any words or phrases that sound awkward. Revise anything that sounds awkward. If no classmate is available, read your report aloud.

Activity 3C Connecting Contrasting Ideas

Use the two statements below to complete a paragraph that begins with the sentence, "All schools should require students to take physical education classes." Use appropriate words to connect the two statements.

- According to one study, the percentage of students who watched television three or more hours on an average school day was 32 percent.

- Researchers studying physical education classes found that students are active for only 16 minutes out of the entire class period.

All schools should require all students to take physical

education classes. _____

_____

_____

_____

_____

_____

_____

_____

_____

_____

Inconsistent Sources

Sources can seem to conflict when they define terms differently. Consider how sources might report the number of students in a high school.

- One says 933: this is the average daily attendance

- One says 1,004: this includes all students expected every day

- One says 1,068: this includes students who are home-schooled and ones studying overseas

When you find sources that seem to conflict, check them carefully to understand why they differ.

LESSON 4 CITATIONS AND QUOTATIONS

Research involves collecting the ideas of others and synthesizing them into something new. This synthesis is very different from **plagiarism,** which is presenting someone else's words as your own. Plagiarism is wrong, and many teachers punish it severely. You can avoid plagiarism if you use

- citations to give credit to your sources
- quotation marks when you use another writer's exact words

Citations

A **citation** is a note in a text that identifies the source of information. In one commonly used format for citations:

- If the author is not identified in the text, his or her last name, or the name of the organization that produced the text, is noted in parentheses at the end of the sentence.
- If the source has page numbers, the page number is also included in the parentheses.

For example, consider this sentence:

> In 1860 and 1861, as slave states left the Union, many antislavery leaders preferred to let them go rather than to start a war to stop them. (Foner, 146).

The citation tells the reader that the information in the sentence came from page 146 of a book by an author named Foner. The author's full name (Eric Foner), the book title *(The Fiery Trial),* and other information about the book should appear in a list of sources at the end of a report called the Works Cited list.

Quotations

If you repeat a statement word-for-word from a source, enclose the words in quotation marks. If you use information from a source but phrase it in your own words, do not use quotation marks.

Activity 4A *Identifying Quotations and Citations*

In the passage below, the information is from an excerpt used in Lesson 2.

1. Underline a direct quotation.

2. Place a check mark beside an indirect quotation.

3. Circle a citation in parentheses.

4. Draw a box around the name of an author that is identified in a sentence rather than in parentheses.

Citations on Tests

Citations may not be required for essays on tests. However, including them is a good habit. By indicating your sources, you can easily go back to them if you need to.

Works Cited Sample

Here is an example of an entry in a Work Cited list for an online government report. The date at the end tells when the researcher read the Web page.

Frieden, Thomas R. Foreward. *Preventing Tobacco Use Among Youth and Young Adults.* Office of the Surgeon General, 2012. Web. 22 Oct. 2012.

Smoking is dangerous. A report published by the Office of the Surgeon General says that cigarettes cause 20 percent of the deaths in the country each year (Frieden). In that same report, Regina Benjamin indicates that breaking the smoking habit is difficult: "Of every three young smokers, only one will quit, and one of those remaining smokers will die from tobacco-related causes."

Activity 4B Using Citations and Quotations

Imagine you are writing a research report about the history of slavery in the United States. The excerpt below is from an essay by Walter B. Hill Jr. published on a federal government website. Use the excerpt to complete the two items that follow it.

> Lincoln made clear the official government position that slavery would be protected where it existed but refused to allow its expansion. The South felt that all of its institutions, in particular slavery, were threatened and challenged the government's position.

1. Write a sentence that uses a direct quotation from the excerpt by Hill. Identify the author in the text.

_____

_____

_____

2. Write a sentence that uses an indirect quotation from the excerpt by Hill. Identify the author in parentheses.

_____

_____

_____

_____

Collaborate with Quotations

Interview a partner about a book the individual has read, and then write a summary of the interview. Include at least two direct quotations and two indirect quotations in your summary.

LESSON 5 HOW TO WRITE A RESEARCH REPORT

Following is a model demonstrating the six steps in writing a research report. Use these six steps to help you write your own essays.

Step 1. Understand the prompt.

Begin by reading the directions closely. The directions that explain what to write about are called a **prompt.**

- The prompt might describe a general topic, such as school discipline codes. You will need to narrow the subject down to a topic you can cover in your report.

- The prompt might already be very well defined. It may come either before or after the sources that will provide the textual evidence you will use in your report.

> **Interpreting the Prompt**
>
> Many students score poorly on tests because they do not read the prompt carefully enough. For example, think of the difference between a prompt that asks you to *describe* your school and one that asks you to *evaluate* your school.

Activity 5A Analyzing the Prompt

Summarize the following prompt in your own words.

Schools have some power to restrict the free speech rights of students. The limits of this power are determined by various court decisions. The development of social media has made the situation more complex. Below are several sources on this topic. Use the information in them to write a report describing how schools should balance the freedom of speech rights of students with other responsibilities of schools.

_____

_____

_____

_____

_____

Step 2. Take notes on the sources.

Whether the sources are provided for you on a test or you find your own, take notes on them with your purpose in mind.

- Underline key statements in the source.

- To help you find the notes later, write a brief note in the margin identifying the point of the underlined text. The following activity includes a model.

> **Another Option for Taking Notes**
>
> For additional ideas about how to organize your notes, see Chapter 2, "Writing an Argumentative Essay," page 15.

Activity 5B Underlining and Adding Notes

Take notes on the following sources by underlining key statements and adding notes in the margin. One note is done for you as a model.

Source 1

"Students and Free Speech,"
from the United States Courts Web Site

In *Tinker v. Des Moines* (1969), the Court stated that students do not <u>"shed their constitutional rights to freedom of speech or expression at the schoolhouse gate."</u> Tinker held that the wearing of armbands by students to protest the Vietnam War was constitutionally protected speech because it was political speech. Political speech is at the heart of the First Amendment and, thus, can only be prohibited if it "substantially disrupts" the educational process.

> *Tinker v. Des Moines*

On the other hand, the Court noted in *Bethel v. Fraser,* 478 U.S. 675, 682 (1986) that "the constitutional rights of students at public school are not automatically, coextensive with the rights of adults." The rights of students are applied "in light of the special characteristics of the school environment," according to the U.S. Supreme Court in *Hazelwood School District v. Kuhlmeier,* 484 U.S. 260, 266 (1988).

Source: "Free Speech and School Conduct." *United States Courts.* Web.

Source 2

School Wins in Doninger v. Niehoff

When Principal Karissa Niehoff cancelled the annual music festival at her Connecticut high school, she angered junior class secretary Avery Doninger. On her blog, Doninger sharply criticized the school administrators for their decision. She called Niehoff at least one offensive name.

The school responded by banning Doninger from serving as class secretary. The administrators argued that Doninger would not work effectively with people she had attacked so harshly. Was the school correct in punishing Doninger? Or did Doninger's free speech rights cover what she said on her own blog on her own time?

The dispute ended up in the federal district court, as the case *Doninger v. Niehoff*. The panel of judges in court sided with the school. The court reasoned that the new technology broke down the distinction between on and off campus. The school was justified in thinking that Doninger's comments could disrupt the workings of student government. According to prior court decisions, schools had the power to restrict student speech in order to make the school run smoothly. Therefore, the administration had a right to prevent this disruption.

Source 3

Student Wins in J. S. v. Blue Mountain School District
from Thomson Reuters Web Site

A federal appeals court in Philadelphia has ruled in favor of two school students who were disciplined in different districts for creating what lawyers called parodies of their principals on the MySpace social network site.

"The U.S. Court of Appeals for the Third Circuit made clear ... that schools cannot punish students for out-of-school speech that does not create a substantial and material disruption in-side the school," said the American Civil Liberties Union, which represented the students.

continued on next page

"I think the message is louder for school officials than it is for the kids," ACLU lawyer Witold Walczak, the organization's Pennsylvania legal director, said Tuesday.

And that message, he said, is that the authority of school officials is less for conduct outside the school than it is for conduct inside.

Terry Snyder, mother of one of the students who was referred to in the legal papers as only "JS," said she disciplined her daughter for her behavior while she was a student in the Blue Mountain School District, in central Pennsylvania north of Reading.

"I punished her for that," said Snyder Tuesday. "I'm the one who should have punished her."

But the school district insisted on a 10-day suspension, and that led to the lawsuit.

Source: "Court Rules for Students in Pennsylvania Cases." *Thomson Reuters.* June 14, 2011.

Source 4

Schools Confront Cyberbullying, by Eddi Trevizo

For two weeks in March, students, teachers, and administrators at Millennium High School in Goodyear were besieged with anonymous Facebook comments ridiculing their work ethic, social status, physical appearance, and sexual relationships. Because of Facebook's online-privacy policies and vague state laws governing such posts, officials were powerless to stop the comments, even though some felt they were disruptive to the school environment.

The Millennium case illustrates the difficulty administrators have in balancing student privacy, the right to freedom of expression, and the need to protect young people from online harassment or bullying. District officials can't counter cyberbullying on Facebook pages. Nationally, concerns over cyberbullying have escalated after several high-profile cases in which teenagers committed suicide after being bullied online.

Source: Trevizo, Eddi. "Free Speech, Social Media Collide at Goodyear School." *Arizona Central.* April 30, 2012. Web.

Step 3. Organize your ideas.

Determine the best order in which to present your ideas. The order should be logical so that readers can easily follow your train of thought. Making an outline before you write your draft will help you organize your ideas.

A research report, like most other types of texts, is organized into three basic parts: The **introduction** should introduce the topic and state it clearly, usually in one paragraph. The **body** should present the research, often in several paragraphs. The **conclusion** should restate the topic and summarize the research. It should give a sense of closure to the writing.

> **Collaborate about Organization**
>
> Before organizing your information, discuss it with a partner. Talking about what you have researched can help you see the best way to organize it.

Activity 5C Organizing Information

Below is an alphabetical list of five presidents who were famous for their military service. Use the list to answer the questions that follow.

Name	Dates Served	Political Party
Eisenhower, Dwight	1953–1961	Republican
Grant, Ulysses	1860–1877	Republican
Jackson, Andrew	1829–1837	Democratic
Kennedy, John	1961–1964	Democratic
Roosevelt, Theodore	1901–1909	Republican

1. If you were organizing a report about these presidents by time period, in what order would you present them?

_____

2. If you were organizing a report about these presidents by political party, which ones would you group together?

_____

Activity 5D Analyzing an Outline

Following is an outline for a research report about the free speech of students. As you read it, mark it as follows:

1. Circle the heading for the portions of the outline that are part of the body.

2. Underline where the research question is stated.

3. Are the main points in the body in logical order? Why or why not?

Sample Outline: Schools, the First Amendment, and Social Media

I. Introduction

    A. The First Amendment protects free speech.

    B. Students do not have complete free speech.

    C. How do schools balance free speech and other issues?

II. Background

    A. *Tinker v. Des Moines* protected student speech that was not disruptive.

    B. *Bethel v. Fraser* upheld restrictions on student speech.

III. Cases About Criticizing Staff

    A. *Doninger v. Niehoff* supported the school.

    B. *J.S. v. Blue Mountain School District* sided with the student.

IV. Stories About Bullying

    A. The Millennium High School example shows students being bullied anonymously.

    B. Schools have the right to stop disruptive comments, but schools cannot get names from social media sites.

V. Conclusion

    A. Schools give students some rights but not all rights.

    B. New technology may make balancing rights and order harder.

Step 4. Write the draft.

Below is a draft of the report. It is based on the outline and the notes taken on the sources.

Activity 5E Analyzing a Draft

Following is the draft of an essay. Mark it as follows:

1. In the margin beside the first sentence, write a phrase to indicate whether you think it is an effective opening line.

2. Write "introduction" beside the introductory paragraph and "conclusion" beside the concluding paragraph.

3. Place a check mark in the margin beside three specific pieces of evidence from the sources.

> **Two Special Sentences**
>
> The first and last sentences of a report are particularly important.
> The first sentence of the introduction should grab the reader's attention.
> The last sentence of the conclusion should leave a strong impression in the reader's mind.

4. Circle three transitional words or phrases.

5. Draw a box around headings that show the organization of the essay.

6. In the margin beside the last sentence, write a phrase to indicate whether you think it is effective.

7. In the margin at the end of the report, write yes, somewhat, or no to evaluate whether this report demonstrates understanding of the subject under investigation.

Sample Draft: Schools, the First Amendment, and Social Media

The First Amendment doesn't mean what it says. It states that "Congress shall make no law . . . abridging the freedom of speech." However, Congress has passed laws that have limited the rights of people to lie to encourage violence, and even to oppose war. Schools has limited the speech of students even more in order to keep order. How has the rise of social media complicated the issue of trying to balance free speech with a good learning environment?

Background

Two important cases show how the Supreme Court tried to limit but not eliminate the free speech rights of students. In 1969, in the case of *Tinker v. Des Moines*, the court sided with students who wore black armbands to school to protest the war in Vietnam. According to the Court, students do not "shed their constitutional rights to freedom of speech or expression at the schoolhouse gate." Schools could restrict student speech only if it "substantially disrupts" learning (United States Courts). In contrast, in 1986, in the case of *Bethel v. Fraser*, the Court allowed schools to restrict student speech. The decision states plainly that "the constitutional rights of students at public school are not automatically, coextensive with the rights of adults" (United States Courts).

Recent Cases

Recent court cases about student use of social media has continued to try to give students some but not all rights. For example, courts rule in cases in which students posted insulting, crude comments on social media sites that criticized school employees. In the case of *J. S. vs. Blue Mountain School District*, the court ruled that the comments did not threaten to disrupt school (Thompson Reuters). On the other hand, in the case of *Doninger v. Niehoff*, a different ruling was made by the court.

continued on next page

continued from previous page

The court agreed with the school that the comments could be disruptive, so the school could punish the student ("School Wins").

Millennium High School in Goodyear, Arizona, showed another problem with trying to punish students for what they say on social media sites. Someone created a page that several students were positing comments on without giving their names. They were bullying and ridiculing other students. The school wanted to stop them. However, the social media company would not release the names of the student posting the comments. The school thought it had a right under Tinker to stop the potentially disruptive comments, but it did not (Trevizo).

Where do these court decisions leave schools? The standard set in the Tinker and Bethel decisions still stand. Students have a right to free speech—but not to disrupt the learning by others. Schools have power to punish students—but not to take away all of their rights. Schools and courts are figuring out how to apply these standards to social network sites. Courts support schools that have punished students even though the behavior took place outside of school—if schools can identify the offenders.

Step 5. Revise your essay.

After you write a draft, read it again. Make revisions to improve it. For example, review the verb in each sentence to see if you can replace it with one that is more precise and descriptive. In the following passage, which underlined phrase sounds stronger and more direct?

> In the case of *J. S. vs. Blue Mountain School District*, the <u>court ruled that the comments</u> did not threaten to disrupt school (Thompson Reuters). On the other hand, in the case of *Doninger v. Niehoff*, <u>a different ruling was made by the court.</u>

The first underlined phrase is in active voice. In **active voice,** the subject performs an action. In this phrase, the focus is on the court making a ruling. However, in the second underlined phrase, the focus is on the ruling that is receiving the action of the court. This phrase is in passive voice. In **passive voice,** the action of the verb is being performed upon the subject. Passive voice verbs often use a form of the verb *be* (such as *is, was,* or *were)* before the main verb.

Active and Passive

Using active voice makes your writing stronger and more direct because it makes clear who is performing an action. However, writers sometimes want to avoid responsibility. "I made a mistake" is active. "Mistakes were made" is passive.

Activity 5F Using Active Voice Verbs

Rewrite each sentence so that it is in active voice:

1. On the other hand, in the case of *Doninger v. Niehoff,* a different ruling was made by the court.

_____

_____

2. The exceptionally good essay was written by me.

_____

_____

3. The paintings by Picasso were studied by our art class.

_____

_____

4. The governor was reelected by the people of the state.

_____

_____

5. The class was taken mostly by sophomores.

_____

_____

6. The vase was broken by the visitor.

_____

_____

7. These truths are held by us to be self-evident.

_____

_____

> ### Collaboration about Passive Voice
>
> Active voice is usually better than passive voice. However, careful writers sometimes use passive voice to focus on the receiver of an action rather than the person doing the action. Discuss with a partner the following sentences. Decide which is active voice and which is passive voice, and how they differ in emphasis.
>
> - The principal handed the award to Carol.
> - Carol accepted the award from the principal.

Step 6. Edit and proofread your essay.

After revising your paper, proofread it carefully, looking for mistakes in spelling, punctuation, and grammar. Compare verbs and subjects, looking for problems such as the one in this sentence from the model:

> The standard set in the Tinker and Bethel decisions still stand.

To make the problem clearer, read the sentence again without the phrase "set in the Tinker and Bethel decisions."

> The standard still stand.

The mistake is that the subject, "standard," is singular, but the verb, "stand," is plural. To agree, both the subject and the verb must be singular or both must be plural, regardless of words between them.

Activity 5G Making Verbs Agree with Subjects

1. Rewrite this sentence correctly: "The standard set in the Tinker and Bethel decisions still stand."

_____

_____

2. Find an example of faulty subject/verb agreement in the introduction of the student model and rewrite it correctly.

_____

_____

3. Find an example of faulty subject/verb agreement in the first paragraph under the heading "Recent Cases" in the student model and rewrite it correctly.

_____

_____

Activity 5H Proofreading an Essay

Correct three other mistakes you see in verb usage, spelling, or punctuation in the first paragraph of the model essay.

LESSON 6 YOU TRY IT

Now it is your turn to write a research report. Use the steps outlined in this chapter to guide you as you write.

Step 1. Understand the prompt.

Step 2. Take notes on sources.

Step 3. Organize your ideas.

Step 4. Write the draft.

Step 5. Revise your essay.

Step 6. Edit and proofread your essay.

Activity 6A *Writing a Research Report*

Write a research report in response to one of the following prompts.

A. Influences on Literature	B. Summer Activities
Harper Lee published *To Kill a Mockingbird* in 1960. The events in the book are set in the 1930s. Conduct research and then write a report that answers this question: How did the historical and cultural setting of the mid-1900s influence the events in *To Kill a Mockingbird?* Use information from at least four sources in your report and use a standard format for citations.	Many high school students have no organized activities to participate in during the summer. Research one aspect of this problem and write a report about possible ways to solve it. Use information from at least four sources in your report and use a standard format for citations.

My writing has . . .	
DEVELOPMENT	❏ a clear question to answer or problem to solve ❏ a topic appropriate to the length of the report
ORGANIZATION	❏ a clear introduction, body, and conclusion ❏ good transitions to maintain the flow of ideas ❏ logical order
EVIDENCE	❏ strong, relevant textual evidence ❏ information from multiple authoritative sources
LANGUAGE & STYLE	❏ precise, appropriate word choice ❏ a formal, objective tone
GRAMMAR, SPELLING, & PUNCTUATION	❏ standard grammar ❏ correct spelling ❏ proper punctuation

Writing a Literary Analysis

A **literary analysis** interprets one or more works of literature. It supports that interpretation with appropriate evidence, such as quotations and other details, from the literature. In addition, a literary analysis often includes facts and informed judgments from other sources, such as biographies of the writer or historical works about the events described in the literature.

> **Types of Literature**
>
> Writing assessments may ask you to read and respond to poetry, drama, or a short story.

LESSON 1 ELEMENTS OF A LITERARY ANALYSIS

A literary analysis essay requires you to look at specific elements of a work of literature. Here are some commonly used literary devices found in stories and poems and how you might be asked to write about them in an essay.

Definitions of Literary Elements	A prompt may ask you to analyze how . . .
Characterization: description of the characters in the story	• characters develop and change • characters advance the plot • characters develop the theme
Plot: events in the story	• events in the story influence the characters • the author uses events to create mystery or tension
Structure: arrangement of lines of poetry or the order in which ideas are presented	• the structure supports the theme
Setting: where and when the events take place	• the setting influences the plot and the characters' choices
Tone: author's attitude toward the writing	• the author's choice of words creates the tone
Point of View: who is narrating the events	• point of view influences the story or poem
Theme: central idea of a text	• the theme is developed, shaped, and refined by specific details • two passages on the same topic or with the same theme are similar or different
Figurative Language: similes, metaphors, allusions	• imagery or sound devices convey meaning

> **Collaboration on Figurative Language**
>
> In a small group, develop three examples of each type of figurative language described below.
>
> • A **simile** is a comparison using the words *like* or *as*. Example: Life is *like* baseball.
>
> • A **metaphor** is a comparison that does not use *like* or *as*. Example: Life is a baseball game.
>
> • An **allusion** is a reference to something well-known that may not be clearly stated or explained. Example: He was a Scrooge when it came to buying clothes. (Scrooge is the character in *A Christmas Carol* famous for not spending money.)

Activity 1A *Understanding Literary Devices*

Choose a work of literature you have read recently. Complete the following tasks to help you analyze the work.

Title: _____

1. Describe the main characters:

_____

_____

_____

2. Summarize the plot:

_____

_____

_____

_____

_____

3. Describe the setting:

_____

_____

4. Identify the tone:

_____

_____

5. Identify the point of view:

_____

_____

6. Explain the theme:

_____

_____

7. Give examples of two types of figurative language used:

_____

_____

_____

LESSON 2 EVIDENCE FROM TEXTS

Before you write an essay, you will be asked to read a work of literature such as a short story or poem. Watch for important details in the writing; underline key sentences that describe the characters and reveal the theme of the work.

When you are done reading, the test may ask you questions about the literature. You may be asked to explain key words or phrases, write a summary, or find evidence to support the main ideas. Answering these questions correctly will help you accurately interpret the literature in your analysis essay.

 Activity 2A Answering Questions About a Work of Literature

Read the following short story and answer the questions that follow.

> **Paying Close Attention**
>
> As you read a work of literature, take notes about anything that strikes you. For example, write down questions about why a character does something or why the writer mentions a specific detail. Comment on figurative language, unusual words, or changes of direction in the plot. Use your notes to help you analyze the text.

The Other Wife, by Colette

TABLE FOR TWO? This way, Monsieur, Madame, there is still a table next to the window, if Madame and Monsieur would like a view of the bay."

Alice followed the maitre d'.

"Oh, yes. Come on, Marc, it'll be like having lunch on a boat on the water . . ."

Her husband caught her by passing his arm under hers.

"We'll be more comfortable over there."

"There? In the middle of all those people? I'd much rather . . ."

"Alice, please."

He tightened his grip in such a meaningful way that she turned around. "What's the matter?"

"Shh . . ." he said softly, looking at her intently, and led her toward the table in the middle.

"What is it, Marc?"

"I'll tell you, darling. Let me order lunch first. Would you like the shrimp? Or the eggs in aspic?"

"Whatever you like, you know that."

They smiled at one another, wasting the precious time of an over-worked maitre d', stricken with a kind of nervous dance, who was standing next to them, perspiring.

"The shrimp," said Marc. "Then the eggs and bacon. And the cold chicken with a lettuce salad. Cream cheese? The house specialty? We'll go with the specialty. Two strong coffees. My chauffeur will be having lunch also, we'll be leaving again at two o'clock. Some cider? No, I don't trust it . . . Dry champagne."

He sighed as if he had just moved an armoire, gazed at the colorless midday sea, at the pearly white sky, then at his wife, whom he found lovely in her little Mercury hat with its large, hanging veil.

continued on next page

---

continued from previous page

"You're looking well, darling. And all this blue water makes your eyes look green, imagine that! And you've put on weight since you've been traveling . . . It's nice up to a point, but only up to a point!"

"Why did you keep me from taking that place next to the window?"

Marc Seguy never considered lying. "Because you were about to sit next to someone I know."

"Someone I don't know?"

"My ex-wife."

She couldn't think of anything to say and opened her blue eyes wider.

"So what, darling? It'll happen again. It's not important."

The words came back to Alice and she asked, in order, the inevitable questions. "Did she see you? Could she see that you saw her? Will you point her out to me?"

"Don't look now, please, she must be watching us . . . The lady with brown hair, no hat, she must be staying in this hotel. By herself, behind those children in red . . ."

"Yes I see."

Hidden behind some broad-brimmed beach hats, Alice was able to look at the woman who, fifteen months ago, had still been her husband's wife.

"Incompatibility," Marc said. "Oh, I mean . . . total incompatibility! We divorced like well-bred people, almost like friends, quietly, quickly. And then I fell in love with you, and you really wanted to be happy with me. How lucky we are that our happiness doesn't involve any guilty parties or victims!"

The woman in white, whose smooth, lustrous hair reflected the light from the sea in azure patches, was smoking a cigarette with her eyes half closed. Alice turned back toward her husband, took some shrimp and butter, and ate calmly. After a moment's silence she asked: "Why didn't you ever tell me that she had blue eyes, too?"

"Well, I never thought about it!"

He kissed the hand she was extending toward the breadbasket and she blushed with pleasure. Dusky and ample, she might have seemed somewhat coarse, but the changeable blue of her eyes and her wavy, golden hair made her look like a frail and sentimental blonde. She vowed overwhelming gratitude to her husband. Immodest without knowing it, everything about her bore the overly conspicuous marks of extreme happiness.

They ate and drank heartily, and each thought the other had forgotten the woman in white. Now and then, however, Alice laughed too loudly, and Marc was careful about his posture, holding his shoulders back, his head up. They waited quite a long time for their coffee, in silence. An incandescent river, the straggled reflection of the invisible sun overhead, shifted slowly across the sea and shone with a blinding brilliance.

"She's still there, you know," Alice whispered.

"Is she making you uncomfortable? Would you like to have coffee somewhere else?"

"No, not at all! She's the one who must be uncomfortable! Besides, she doesn't exactly seem to be having a wild time, if you could see her . . ."

continued on next page

continued from previous page

"I don't have to. I know that look of hers."

"Oh, was she like that?"

He exhaled his cigarette smoke through his nostrils and knitted his eyebrows. "Like that? No. To tell you honestly, she wasn't happy with me."

"Oh, really now!"

"The way you indulge me is so charming, darling . . . It's crazy . . . You're an angel . . . You love me . . . I'm so proud when I see those eyes of yours. Yes, those eyes . . . She . . . I just didn't know how to make her happy, that's all. I didn't know how."

"She's just difficult!"

Alice fanned herself irritably, and cast brief glances at the woman in white, who was smoking, her head resting against the back of the cane chair, her eyes closed with an air of satisfied lassitude.

Marc shrugged his shoulders modestly.

"That's the right word," he admitted. "What can you do? You have to feel sorry for people who are never satisfied. But we're satisfied . . . Aren't we, darling?"

She did not answer. She was looking furtively, and closely, at her husband's face, ruddy and regular; at his thick hair, threaded here and there with white silk; at his short, well-cared-for hands; and doubtful for the first time, she asked herself, "What more did she want from him?"

And as they were leaving, while Marc was paying the bill and asking for the chauffeur and about the route, she kept looking, with envy and curiosity, at the woman in white, this dissatisfied, this difficult, this superior woman. . .

Part A

What does the word lassitude mean in these lines from the text?

> "Alice fanned herself irritably, and cast brief glances at the woman in white, who was smoking, her head resting against the back of the cane chair, her eyes closed with an air of satisfied lassitude."

a. excitement

b. indifference

c. anxiousness

d. anger

Part B

Which words or phrases from the text in Part A best help the reader understand the meaning of the word *lassitude*?

a. fanned herself irritably

b. cast brief glances

c. satisfied

d. head resting . . . her eyes closed

Vocabulary

A set of "selected response" questions can help you understand what you have just read. Some tests present them in two parts. These questions ask you to define a key word from the story. The second question asks you to provide context clues that helped you understand the definition.

Activity 2B *Identifying Key Ideas*

Use your reading of "The Other Wife" to answer the following questions.

Part A

Which of the following best describes Alice's response to the encounter with Marc's ex-wife?

  a. She is not affected by the encounter.

  b. She is curious about Marc's ex-wife, and then feels dissatisfied with her marriage.

  c. She is thankful for Marc, and feels hatred toward his ex-wife.

  d. As she learns more about his ex-wife, she falls more in love with Marc.

Part B

Select three pieces of evidence from "The Other Wife" that support the answer to Part A.

  a. "They smiled at one another, wasting the precious time of an over-worked maitre d'. . ."

  b. "He kissed the hand she was extending toward the bread basket and she blushed with pleasure."

  c. "She vowed overwhelming gratitude to her husband. Immodest without knowing it, everything about her bore the overly conspicuous marks of extreme happiness."

  d. "The words came back to Alice and she asked, in order, the inevitable questions. 'Did she see you? Could she see that you saw her? Will you point her out to me?'"

  e. ". . . each thought the other had forgotten the woman in white. Now and then, however, Alice laughed too loudly, and Marc was careful about his posture, holding his shoulders back, his head up."

  f. "She did not answer. She was looking furtively, and closely, at her husband's face . . . doubtful for the first time, she asked herself, 'What more did she want from him?'"

  g. ". . . she kept looking, with envy and curiosity, at the woman in white, this dissatisfied, this difficult, this superior woman. . ."

> ### Key Idea
>
> The first of a pair of questions might ask you to identify the key idea in a text. A second question might ask you to identify one or more statements that provide evidence for your choice.

> ### Draw Evidence from Literary Texts
>
> Writers often indicate their key ideas through the details they choose to include. In detective stories and mysteries, the plot often turns on one little piece of information. If a detail seems odd or unnecessary, ask yourself why the writer took the time to create it.

LESSON 3 HOW TO WRITE A LITERARY ANALYSIS ESSAY

A literary analysis essay will ask you to look for specific elements of the text, such as the theme, the characters, the point of view, or the word choice. You will be required to supply textual evidence to support your analysis of the story. The following will help you break down the process of writing a literary analysis into manageable steps.

Step 1. Understand the prompt.

The directions for writing an essay are called the **prompt.** The verbs in it tell you what to do. Here is an example of a prompt:

> Analyze the characters of Marc, Alice, and Marc's ex-wife in the story "The Other Wife." Base your analysis on what the characters say and do and on what the narrator says about the characters' thoughts and actions. Discuss which character changes the most during the story and what causes the character to change. Be sure to include specific evidence from the text.

Activity 3A Analyzing a Prompt

In the prompt above, underline two key words or phrases in each sentence. Then finish the following statements:

1. In my literary analysis, I must

_____

_____

2. The kinds of details I should include in my essay are

_____

_____

Step 2. Take notes on the texts.

As you read "The Other Wife," you may have underlined some important sentences or written some notes in the margins. Now you should return to the story with the prompt in mind.

- Look for clues that reveal the personality of each character.
- Find specific examples of the characters' words and actions.
- Organize your notes, possibly using a graphic organizer.

The chart on the next page contains examples of graphic organizers that fit with different writing prompts.

Notes on Literary Texts

In nonfiction, the entire text might be from one point of view–that of the author. In short stories and novels, characters each have their own point of view. You may not be sure if any of the characters represent the author's point of view. As part of your notes, keep track of which character is responsible for the information.

Words in the Prompt	Type of Graphic Organizer	Model
• Compare and contrast two texts • Analyze how an author transforms source material from an older text	Venn diagram	
• Summarize the plot • Analyze how a character changes	flow chart	
• Determine the theme • Describe a character	web diagram	
• Analyze characters, tone, or word choice	two-column chart	

Activity 3B Organizing Notes

The chart below includes notes from "The Other Wife." Complete the chart by following these steps.

1. For each character, add another entry to the Description/Evidence column.

2. Under the Degree of Change column, fill in the empty cells for Marc and Alice.

Character	Description/Evidence	Degree of Change
Marc's ex-wife	• "smooth, lustrous hair" • "blue eyes"	No change: we know very little about her, but we see how her presence affects the other characters.
Marc	• Avoids ex-wife • Has never talked about ex-wife with Alice—"Why didn't you ever tell me that she had blue eyes, too?" • Seems controlling—orders lunch for Alice; hints that she shouldn't put on too much weight	
Alice	• Appears to be happy—"bore the overly conspicuous marks of extreme happiness" • Very curious about Marc's ex-wife—Alice keeps looking at the ex-wife during lunch. • At the end, she doesn't answer when Marc comments that they are satisfied in their marriage.	

Step 3. Write a thesis statement.

Once you've gathered notes, you should write a thesis statement. The **thesis statement** should clearly state the central idea of your literary analysis. It will guide your writing, so it should fit both the prompt and your notes.

Activity 3C Write a Thesis Statement

Finish the sentence to write a strong thesis statement or write your own thesis statement on the lines provided.

1. In the story "The Other Wife," a chance encounter with Marc's ex-wife reveals

_____

_____

2. Thesis Statement:

_____

_____

Step 4. Organize your ideas.

Next, think about how you will organize your notes and your thesis statement into a cohesive essay. As you may already know, essays have three main parts: an introduction, a body, and a conclusion.

The introduction should include the title of the text and the author. You may want to summarize the work in one or two sentences. You should also include your thesis statement.

In the body of your essay, develop your thesis statement by stating your conclusions about the literature. How you organize these main points will depend on the prompt you have been given. Since this prompt asks you to analyze the characters, one logical way to organize your essay is by writing a paragraph about each of the characters. The prompt also requires that you discuss which character changes the most, so you might organize the characters from the least amount of change to the greatest degree of change.

The conclusion of the essay brings the writing together in a satisfying way. You may include a final thought. You may also restate your thesis statement using different words.

Step 5. Develop a complete outline.

Before writing your essay, develop an outline to organize the main ideas and supporting details.

Ways to Organize a Literary Analysis

- Comparison/contrast: describe all similarities/ differences of one text and then the other; or, describe one similarity shared by both texts and then one difference between the two texts

- Summaries, Plot analysis, Character analysis: explain examples in chronological order

- Analysis of Word Choice or Theme: organize examples in order of importance (usually least to most important)

Activity 3D Analyzing an Outline

Use work you have done for previous activities to help you complete the following outline for a literary analysis essay about "The Other Wife."

1. Fill in the thesis statement next to the word Thesis Statement and also under point B of I. Introduction.

2. Fill in subpoints 1 and 2 under points A, B, and C of II. Body.

3. Restate the thesis statement under point B of III. Conclusion.

Sample Outline: A Chance Encounter Changes Everything

Thesis Statement:

_____

_____

I.   **Introduction**

    A. Alice and Marc accidently run into Marc's ex-wife while eating lunch at a hotel.

    B. _____

       _____

II. **Body**

    A. Very little is revealed about Marc's ex-wife, but her presence spurs the conflict of the story.

       1. _____

          _____

       2. _____

          _____

    B. Marc appears to be a loving husband, but his behavior hints that he may be very demanding.

       1. _____

          _____

       2. _____

          _____

    C. Alice's attitude toward her marriage changes during the story.

       1. _____

continued on next page

continued from previous page

2. _____

_____

III. Conclusion

A. The focus of the story is Alice's changing attitude toward her marriage.

B. _____

_____

Including Textual Evidence

The body of your outline should include specific evidence from the text. Evidence may include direct quotations enclosed in quotation marks or paraphrases of the text.

Step 6. Write the draft.

Because you've taken good notes and developed a complete outline, writing your essay will not be difficult. Simply add a few more details to your basic outline. You will also want to include good transitional words and phrases so that the writing flows logically.

Activity 3E Analyzing a Model Essay

As you read the essay, complete the following tasks:

1. Underline the thesis statement in the introduction.

2. In the body of the essay, place a check in the margin beside three specific pieces of evidence from the story.

3. Underline two transitional phrases.

4. Identify the conclusion in the margin.

Citations in Literary Analysis

In some writing assignments, you will need to identify your sources in your text. For examples showing how to do this, see Chapter 4, Lesson 4, "Citations and Quotations," pages 57–58.

In literary analysis, all of the citations may come from one text. If so, only the page number is needed. If the work is short, such as a one-page poem, no citation may be needed at all.

Sample Draft: A Chance Encounter Changes Everything

In just a few pages of text, "The Other Wife" reveals three characters: Marc, Marcs wife Alice, and Marcs ex-wife. Colette must be a good writer to communicate a lot about the characters in such a short story. Because what seems to be a simple story is really a very complex one. One character walks away from the encounter changed—that character is Alice.

Very little is revealed about Marc's ex-wife, but her presence spurs the conflict in the story. We are told she has "smooth lustrous hair" she sits with her eyes closed in "satisfied lassitude." When Alice says that she doesn't look very happy, Marc claims to remember "that look of hers." Marc says their marriage broke up because he couldn't make her happy. Although we know very little about her, this character, who never speaks, impacts the lives of Marc and Alice.

The narrator reveals Marc's character only through what he says and does. Clearly, he wants to ignore his ex-wife. He has never talked about her, because Alice says, "Why didn't you ever tell me that she had blue eyes, too?" Marc seems to take the blame for their divorce. He says, "I just didn't know how to make her happy." However, although Marc appears to be a loving husband, there are hints that he may be demanding and difficult to please. He takes control of lunch, steering Alice away from his ex-wife, and he orders their food. He hints that Alice shouldn't put on too much weight. These little things give the reader a sense that maybe the ex-wife wasn't the one who was difficult to please.

The character who changes the most during the story is Alice. The narrator reveals how her thoughts and actions change during the story. At the beginning of the story, Alice seems very in love with Marc. She is inordinately proud when he complements her and blushes happily when he kisses her hand. Alice's "entire person revealed overconspicuous signs of extreme happiness." The couple seems too happy to be real.

Over time, the ex-wife's presence causes Alice to doubt. Whether she is satisfied with her marriage. She is very curious about the woman because she continues to look at her during lunch. Although Marc showers Alice with compliments and claims that he couldn't succeed in making his ex-wife happy. At the end of the story Marc says, "As for us, we're so happy . . . Aren't we, darling?" However, Alice doesn't reply. She feels "dubious for the first time." She watches the ex-wife with envy. This unknown woman seems somehow superior to Alice.

The focus of this short short story is the evolution of Alice. Before the chance encounter with Marc's ex-wife, she is content and happy in her marriage. Afterward, she begins to question whether she is too easily pleased with her husband. She wonders if there is something lacking. In the end the reader is also left wondering what will become of Marc and Alice.

Step 7. Revise your essay.

After you write a draft, revise it to make the content more specific, the ideas more clear, and the writing flow more smoothly. Notice how easy this sentence from the story is to read.

> Alice fanned herself irritably, and cast brief glances at the woman in white, who was smoking, <u>her head resting against the back of the cane chair,</u> <u>her eyes closed with an air of satisfied lassitude.</u>

One reason the sentence is smooth is that the two underlined phrases beginning "her head" and "her eyes" have the same structure.

Type of Word	First Phrase	Second Phrase
Possessive pronoun	her	her
Noun	head	eyes
Phrase that includes two prepositional phrases	resting • against the back • of the chair	closed • with an air • of satisfied lassitude

Two or more phrases or sentences that have the same kind of word or group of words, grammatically speaking, have **parallel structure.** Using parallel structure can make your writing flow smoothly. Here are some examples of faulty and good parallel structure.

Faulty Parallel Structure: Rosie's favorite sports are <u>swimming,</u> <u>water-skiing,</u> and to go <u>horseback riding</u>.

Good Parallel Structure: Rosie's favorite sports are <u>swimming,</u> <u>water-skiing,</u> and <u>horseback riding.</u>

Faulty Parallel Structure: The athletes were not only <u>energetic,</u> but also <u>they had a great deal of enthusiasm.</u>

Good Parallel Structure: The athletes were not only <u>energetic,</u> but also <u>enthusiastic.</u>

Parallel Structure in Famous Phrases

Many famous phrases get their strength from their parallel structure. These examples are from Abraham Lincoln:

- "of the people, by the people, for the people"

- "with malice toward none, with charity for all, with firmness in the right"

- "You can fool all of the people some of the time, and some of the people all of the time, but you cannot fool all of the people all of the time."

Activity 3F Using Parallel Structure

Rewrite the following sentence from the student model so that it uses parallel structure.

> He takes control of lunch, steering Alice away from his ex-wife and he orders their food.

_____

_____

_____

_____

Editing Strategy
....

Check for parallel structure by skimming your paper, pausing at the words *and* and *or*. Check on each side of these words to see whether the items joined are parallel. If not, consider making them so.

Activity 3G Revising the Model Essay

Complete the following tasks to edit the model essay:

1. Cross out a sentence in the introduction that doesn't fit with the main idea of the paragraph.

2. Find a sentence that uses the pronoun *we* and rewrite it using a more formal style.

3. Add a transitional word or phrase to help the ideas flow together better.

Step 8. Edit and proofread your essay.

Once you've made your final revisions to the content and the style of your essay, read it once again. This time, focus on and correct any errors in grammar, punctuation, and spelling.

For example, read the following sentences from the student model. What errors do you notice in the underlined phrases?

> Over time, the ex-wife's presence causes Alice to doubt. <u>Whether she is satisfied with her marriage.</u> She is very curious about the woman because she continues to look at her during lunch. <u>Although Marc showers Alice with compliments and claims that he couldn't succeed in making his ex-wife happy.</u>

The thought "Whether she is satisfied with her marriage" appears to be a sentence because it begins with a capital letter and ends with a period. However, it is incomplete. Both a subject and verb are missing. It is a sentence fragment. You can eliminate sentence fragments by

- adding a subject, a verb, or both a subject and a verb

Example: *Alice wonders* whether she is satisfied with her marriage.

- joining a dependent clause with an independent one

independent clause

Example: *Over time, the ex-wife's presence causes Alice to doubt*

dependent clause

whether she is satisfied with her marriage.

Activity 3H Correcting Sentence Fragments

Rewrite the following fragments as complete sentences:

1. although Marc showers Alice with compliments and claims that he couldn't succeed in making his ex-wife happy

_____

_____

2. overwhelming gratitude to her husband

_____

_____

3. waited a long time for their coffee in silence

_____

_____

Collaboration on Fragments

Make a list of three fragments that are missing verbs and three fragments that are missing subjects. Exchange lists with another student. Rewrite the fragments you receive as complete sentences.

Activity 3I Proofreading an Essay

Complete the following tasks to proofread the model essay. Make your corrections in the margin next to the model.

1. Find and change a misspelled word.

2. Find and rewrite one run-on sentence.

3. Insert two missing apostrophes in the introduction.

LESSON 4 YOU TRY IT

Now it is your turn to write a literary analysis. Use the steps outlined in this chapter and listed to the right.

Activity 4A *Writing a Literary Analysis*

Choose one of the following prompts and write a literary analysis using the steps outlined in this chapter. Then use the checklist to make sure your writing conforms to the Characteristics of Good Writing.

A. Comparing Characters	B. Analyzing a Theme
After reading "The Other Wife," read "My Last Duchess" by Robert Browning. Compare how the husband in each work is characterized. Discuss how point of view influences characterization.	Choose a work of literature you have read recently and write an essay analyzing how the theme of the work is developed through the plot, characters, point of view, and/ or word choice.

> ### Steps for Writing a Literary Analysis
>
> 1. Understand the prompt.
> 2. Take notes on the sources.
> 3. Write a thesis statement.
> 4. Organize your ideas.
> 5. Develop a complete outline.
> 6. Write the draft.
> 7. Revise your essay.
> 8. Edit and proofread your essay.

Use the following checklist to edit your essay.

My writing has . . .	
DEVELOPMENT	❑ a clear thesis statement ❑ strong supporting points ❑ addressed all the requirements of the prompt
ORGANIZATION	❑ a clear introduction, body, and conclusion ❑ good transitions ❑ logical order
EVIDENCE	❑ strong, relevant textual evidence ❑ direct quotations or paraphrased information from other texts
LANGUAGE & STYLE	❑ precise, appropriate word choice ❑ a formal, objective tone
GRAMMAR, SPELLING, & PUNCTUATION	❑ standard grammar ❑ correct spelling ❑ proper punctuation

Writing a Narrative

A **narrative** is a text that tells a story. The story can be either true or imagined, but it is always based on a problem, a situation, or an observation.

LESSON 1 POINT OF VIEW

Narratives come in many forms. Scientists, historians, journalists, and writers of fiction all use narratives to tell how something happened. Following are some examples of narratives:

- a novel such as *Harry Potter and the Sorcerer's Stone,* by J. K. Rowling

- a chapter in a book telling the story of Rosa Parks and the Montgomery Bus Boycott

- a science fiction short story you wrote about the two weeks a space alien hid in your garage

- a one-page account of your ongoing conflict with another student at summer camp

> ### Pronoun Clues and Point of View
> A first-person narrator often uses *I, we, me, us, my,* and *our.* A third-person narrator often uses *he, she, they, his, her, their,* and *them.*

The person telling a story is the narrator. If the narrator participates in the events and describes what happens from his or her point of view, the story is a first-person narrative. If the narrator is not a participant, but is telling readers about other people, the story is a third-person narrative.

Activity 1A *Identifying the Point of View*

Place a checkmark in the column to indicate whether each passage is written in the first person or the third person. Write one or more clue words that you used to make your choice.

Passage	First Person	Third Person	Clue Words
1. I shook in horror as I watched my friend Juan walk up to the house. What was he thinking?			
2. Juan walked briskly up to the house. As he did, he thought about the dangers he might face. He was ready.			
3. When two women began their trip, they tried hard to get along.			
4. We understood that we needed to cooperate with each other.			

LESSON 2 NARRATIVE TECHNIQUES

Narrative writers use a variety of techniques to describe experiences, explain why events happened, and to portray characters. For example:

- **Dialogue** consists of words spoken by characters in the story. These words are enclosed in quotation marks. Dialogue helps characters come alive for readers.

- **Description** includes specific details about people, things, and events. These details help the reader imagine what the writer is portraying.

- **Reflection** occurs when a character or the narrator thinks about and comments on what has happened. Reflection helps the readers understand how characters view events in the narrative.

- **Multiple plot lines** are different streams of events that are woven together into one story. A romance might describe the lives of two separate individuals who finally meet and fall in love.

> ### Pacing
>
> A skilled writer of narrative controls the pacing. **Pacing** is how quickly events occur in a story. In a fast-paced story, events rush by. In a slow-paced story, the writer takes more time for description and reflection. Writers often adjust the pacing as a way to control the tension in the story.

Activity 2A Identifying Techniques

In the margin of the following paragraph, write the following:

1. "dialogue" next to two examples of dialogue

2. "description" next to two descriptive words or phrases

3. "reflection" next to a comment showing reflection

4. "second plot" next to the start of a second plot line

"Aren't you Ludwig von Beethoven? The most greatest composer of classical music who ever lived?" I stammered. The wild-haired, intense man stared at me quizzically. Then my three years of studying German suddenly paid off. I repeated my questions, this time in German. He nodded and replied in uncertain English with a heavy German accent, "Yah—and yah." Why had the time machine sent me to see Beethoven? It had just sent me to meet Johnny Cash, the greatest country singer of all time. Was a pattern emerging?

While I was trying to explain to Beethoven where—and when—I had come from, strange events were continuing to occur back in the world I had left. Mick Jagger, the wild-haired, intense singer of the greatest rock band ever, the Rolling Stones (sorry, Beatles!), suddenly vanished while onstage in the midst of a concert. Poof! Just disappeared. Ludwig and I were about to get a visitor.

LESSON 3 SEQUENCE OF EVENTS

As the writer, you decide the order in which to present the events in a narrative.

- Presenting events in the order they occurred helps readers follow the story easily. This type of organization is called **chronological order.**

- Starting in the middle of a dramatic event can be a good way to grab the attention of the readers.

- Starting with the final result of a series of events encourages the reader to focus on the process that lead up to the result.

Whichever order you use, you need to make your text coherent. **Coherent** means that each idea is connected to the one before and after it. In the example below, the first two sentences are linked because "They" refers back to "The Tigers." The second and third sentences are linked by the repetition of the word "celebrated."

> *The Tigers* had won the game. *They* celebrated, of course. Like their coach, though, they celebrated quietly.

You can often connect ideas by using transition words such as those shown in the chart below.

Selecting Events

One of a writer's first decisions is to select which events to include. For example, on most days what you ate for breakfast might be unimportant. However, if you ate something unusual that reflected a change in your life, breakfast might be a significant event.

Connection	Words and Phrases to Make Connections			
Additional Information	in addition	furthermore	moreover	as well
Example	for example	for instance	specifically	namely
Comparison	similarly	in the same way	likewise	coincidentally
Contrast	however	nevertheless	in contrast	on the other hand
Chronology	before	meanwhile	at the same time	prior
	next	then	later	soon
Result	thus	therefore	as a result	consequently
Summary	finally	in conclusion	hence	to summarize

Activity 3A *Writing a Coherent Paragraph*

Write a narrative paragraph. Use at least four of the words in the chart above to make your writing coherent.

_____

_____

_____

LESSON 4 DESCRIPTIVE LANGUAGE

When you write, choose clear, vivid words to express exactly what you mean.

- Use precise words and phrases rather than general ones. *Bone-chilling* conveys more information than *pretty cold.*

- Use details that tell something significant about a person, thing, or event. Noting that a man has a habit of not looking people in the eye might suggest he is nervous.

- Use **sensory words,** words that appeal to the five senses: sight, hearing, taste, smell, and touch. Phrases such as *shockingly bright* or *stinky as week-old fish* impress your ideas on readers.

Finding Vivid Words

Use the thesaurus feature of your word processor to suggest vivid words you can use to replace vague words. Keep a list of new words you see in your reading or hear people say. To help you learn these new words, use them as soon as you can find a time that is appropriate.

Activity 4A Using Precise Words and Phrases

For each general word, write two words or phrases that are more precise.

General Word	More Precise Words or Phrases	
1. road		
2. said		
3. big		
4. slowly		

Activity 4B Using Sensory Language

Write a one-paragraph narrative about an imaginary conflict between two famous people, real or imaginary. Include details that appeal to four of the five senses.

_____

_____

_____

_____

_____

_____

LESSON 5 CONCLUSION

Like other types of writing, a narrative ends with a conclusion. In a narrative, the conclusion typically gives the reader a sense that the story is complete. The conclusion

- should follow from the rest of the narrative, wrapping up any loose ends
- might include reflections on what happened in the narrative, putting the story into a broader context

In a text that is only a page or two long, the conclusion might be only a sentence. In a twenty-chapter novel, the conclusion might be the last chapter.

Collaboration About a Conclusion

If you are having trouble writing a strong conclusion, talk about what you might write with a classmate. If no classmate is available, pretend you are talking with a friend. Many people find that talking aloud helps them clarify what to write.

Activity 5A Writing a Conclusion

Write a one-paragraph conclusion for a narrative retelling an incident from a well-known story, such as a fairy tale or a famous historical event.

Incident: _____

_____

_____

_____

_____

_____

_____

_____

_____

_____

_____

_____

_____

_____

_____

_____

LESSON 6 HOW TO WRITE A NARRATIVE ESSAY

Following is a model demonstrating the six steps in writing a narrative essay. Use these six steps to help you in writing your own essays.

Step 1. Understand the prompt.

The directions for writing a narrative essay are called the **prompt.**

Activity 6A Analyzing the Prompt

Read the following prompt and then list three important features that your essay should include.

Write a fictional first-person narrative based on the incident described in the source provided below. In the source, Benjamin Franklin describes an event from his boyhood. While you can create dialogue and other details from your imagination, your story should be consistent with Franklin's account of the event.

1. _____

2. _____

3. _____

Step 2. Take notes on the sources.

Below is an excerpt from *Autobiography* by Benjamin Franklin. Use it to practice taking notes.

Activity 6B Taking Notes

Read the following excerpt once so that you understand the basic story. Then reread it, underlining key ideas and adding comments alongside the text to help you analyze the development of the narrative.

> **Help with Research**
>
> For help with evaluating sources and taking notes, see Writing an Argumentative Essay, page 21.

Source 1

Autobiography
by Benjamin Franklin

At ten years old, I was taken home to assist my father in his business, which was that of a candle maker. . . . Accordingly, I was employed in cutting wick for the candles, filling the dipping mold and the molds for poured candles, working in the shop, going on errands, etc. I disliked the trade, and had a strong inclination to be a sailor, but my father was against that idea.

However, living near the water, I was much in and about it. I learned early to swim well and to manage boats. When in a boat or canoe with other boys, I was often allowed to be in charge, especially in any case of difficulty. I was generally a leader among the boys, and sometimes led them into scrapes, of which I will mention one instance, as it shows early evidence of public spirit.

There was a salt marsh that bordered part of the millpond where we used to fish for minnows. By means of all our trampling, the edge of the marsh was a muddy quagmire. My proposal was to build a wharf there fit for us to stand upon. I showed my comrades a large heap of stones, which were intended for a new house near the marsh, and which would very well suit our purpose. In the morning, when the workmen were gone, I assembled a number of my play-fellows. Working diligently, sometimes two or three to a stone, we carried all the stones away and built our little wharf.

The next morning the workmen were surprised to find the stones missing, and they found them in our wharf. Inquiry was made about who had removed the stones and we were discovered. Several of us were scolded by our fathers; and though I pleaded the usefulness of the work, my father convinced me that nothing was useful if it was not honest.

Step 3. Organize your ideas.

Create an outline of the basic events in the story as described by Franklin. Include notes that describe the tone of what happened.

Timelines for Narratives

For a narrative essay, you might use a timeline instead of an outline. A timeline will help you keep events in order.

Sample Outline: A Lesson Learned

I. **The Setting**
   A. Benjamin's father is angry. Emphasize how angry he is.
   B. Benjamin is working for his father, helping make candles. Point out that Benjamin knows he cannot escape his father's anger.

II. **Franklin and His Father Talk**
   A. Benjamin's father asks if the boy stole stones that were to be used to build a new house. Indicate that the father already is convinced he knows what happened.
   B. Benjamin tries to defend himself. He argues that the boys took the stones for a good purpose, to build a wharf.
   C. Benjamin's father has no interest in hearing his son's arguments.

III. **Franklin Learns a Lesson**
   A. Benjamin's father tells his son that nothing good can come from evil. Emphasize that this is a lesson the father wants his son to learn.
   B. Benjamin decides to accept his father's point of view rather than argue with him.

Activity 6C Analyzing the Outline

On the outline above, make the following notes:

1. Write "introduction," "body," or "conclusion" in the margin beside each of the three main sections.

2. Circle at least two examples of notes that indicate the tone the writer wanted to express.

3. Write "climax" in the margin beside the place where the conflict is resolved.

4. Write "reflection" in the margin beside the place where Benjamin reflects on what has happened.

Step 4. Write the draft.

*Using your notes and your outline, write your essay. The following
sample draft includes errors that you will correct in later activities.*

Sample Draft: A Lesson Learned

"Benjamin!"

    I could here the iron in my father's voice. It sent a swift
dagger through my heart. It was a tone reserved for only the
most serious crimes—a stern scolding was at hand. I knew
from experience that it was better to stand up and take my
punishment than to run away. Quickly, I turned from my
work cutting wicks for candles. His face was read as heated
coals.

    "Benjamin, did you steal the stones intended for the new
house by the marsh? The workmen found them in the water
near the shore where you and the other boys play. What do
you have to say about this?" he queried.

    I studied the floor near his feet as I silently considered my
argument. Finally, I met his flashing eyes.

    "Yes, Father, we did take the stones, but it was for a good
purpose. With the stones, we built a wharf. You know how
difficult it is to fish when the shore is muddy. The stones
allowed us to catch more fish and thereby helped provide our
families with food. It was really rather good and useful . . ."

    My father silenced me with an upraised hand.

    "Enough, Benjamin! I'll hear none of your arguments. You
stole the rocks from the man who owns the house. You came
by those rocks dishonestly. It matters not to what purpose
you put them—weather good or bad. Doing evil can never
result in good. Is this clear?"

    Pushing back the counterarguments swirling around in
my head, I gulped and meekly replied, "Yes, Father."

Activity 6D Evaluating the Draft

Mark the following comments on the draft:

1. Circle two transition words that connect sentences effectively.

2. Underline three examples of precise words or phrases.

3. Place a check mark in the margin beside two examples of sensory language.

Step 5. Revise your narrative.

After you write a draft, read it again carefully. Make revisions to improve the effectiveness of the writing. For example, check pronouns to see that their meaning is clear. In the following paragraph from the model, circle the three uses of the pronoun *it*.

> "Benjamin!"
>
> I could here the iron in my father's voice. It sent a swift dagger through my heart. It was a tone reserved for only the most serious crimes—a stern scolding was at hand. I knew from experience that it was better to stand up and take my punishment than to run away. Quickly, I turned from my work cutting wicks for candles. . . .

Collaboration About Pronouns

Since you know what you want to say in your writing, you may not notice pronouns that do not have clear antecedents. Ask a friend to read what you write and point out any pronouns that are unclear.

What does the word *It* used in the second sentence of the second paragraph refer to? The ironlike quality of the voice? The father's voice? The reference is unclear. Pronouns such as *it, he,* or *she* replace an earlier noun. The noun that a pronoun refers to is called an **antecedent.** In this case, the sentence would be much clearer if the writer replaces the vague and overused pronoun *it* with a more specific word or phrase.

> I could hear the iron in my father's voice. The harsh sound sent a swift dagger through my heart.

Activity 6E Correcting Vague Pronouns

Rewrite the following sentence. Replace "it" with a more specific word or phrase.

> I thought about tricking my father by lying about where I had been, but it would never work.

_____

_____

_____

Step 6. Edit and proofread your narrative.

After you write a draft, read it again carefully. Make corrections to improve the effectiveness of the writing. You should follow norms and conventions regarding spelling, punctuation, grammar, and usage. What spelling mistake occurs in the following sentence from the model narrative?

> It matters not to what purpose you put them—weather good
> or bad.

The word *weather* is used incorrectly in this sentence. It should be replaced with *whether. Weather* means "atmospheric conditions"; *whether* means "if it is." This is a good example of words that are easily confused. Other examples include *accept/except, advice/advise, it's/its,* and *their/there/they're.* Computer spell-check programs will not catch these types of errors. Proofread your writing carefully to make sure you have chosen the correct word.

Activity 6F Spelling Words Correctly

1. Find a misspelled word in the first sentence of the first paragraph of the student model. Cross it out and write it correctly both in the model and on the line below.

_____

_____

_____

2. Find a misspelled word in the last sentence of the first paragraph of the student model. Cross it out and write it correctly both in the model and on the line below.

_____

_____

_____

Correct Spelling

About 80 percent of words in English follow regular spelling rules. Learning these rules, then, can help you spell most words. Only about 300 English words are truly difficult for most people to spell. This is a small enough number that you can study and master them.

LESSON 7 YOU TRY IT

Now it is your turn to write a narrative. Use the steps outlined in this chapter and listed to the right.

Activity 7A *Writing a Narrative*

Choose one of the following prompts and write a narrative in response to it.

Writing a Narrative Essay

1. Understand the prompt.

2. Take notes on sources.

3. Organize your ideas.

4. Write the draft.

5. Revise your narrative.

6. Edit and proofread your narrative.

A. Writing a Historical Narrative	B. Writing a Sequel
Write an imaginative narrative of a historical event based on a summary of the event found in reliable sources. Use your imagination to create dialogue or description, but what you create should be consistent with the facts you find.	Select a short story from a textbook, library book, or online source. Write a one-page sequel to it, focusing on what happens to one of the characters in the story.

	My writing has . . .
DEVELOPMENT	❐ a clear experience or event to tell ❐ narrative techniques to develop experiences, events, and characters
ORGANIZATION	❐ a problem, situation, or observation to engage the reader ❐ a clear introduction, body, and conclusion ❐ good transitions to maintain the flow of ideas ❐ events that build on one another to create a coherent whole
EVIDENCE	❐ well-chosen details ❐ well-structured event sequences
LANGUAGE & STYLE	❐ precise words and phrases ❐ telling details ❐ sensory language
GRAMMAR, SPELLING, & PUNCTUATION	❐ standard grammar ❐ correct spelling ❐ proper punctuation

Tips for Success

LESSON 1 TEN TIPS FOR QUICK REVISION

You may not have much time to revise an essay on a test. As a result, you will want to decide quickly what to fix. Here is a list of actions to take.

❐ 1. Reread your main idea carefully. It should be stated precisely and clearly.

❐ 2. Compare your introduction and your conclusion. They should both address the main idea.

❐ 3. Be sure your body paragraphs have enough details, such as relevant evidence, well-chosen facts, precise words, and sensory language.

❐ 4. Check for appropriate and varied transitions between paragraphs and between sentences.

❐ 5. Read your essay silently, but slowly, word-by-word, as if you were giving a speech. Revise any awkward words or phrases.

❐ 6. Look for words you might have omitted or written twice.

❐ 7. Check the style and tone of the essay. Usually, you should use a formal style and objective tone.

❐ 8. Check that each pronoun refers clearly to a noun and is used correctly.

❐ 9. Insert commas where they are necessary. Delete commas where they are not.

❐ 10. Correct any misspelled words. If you are writing your essay on a computer, some of these may be highlighted by the word processing program.

Types of Main Ideas

Depending on the type of essay you are writing your main idea might be a

• claim to support

• topic to examine

• situation to explain

• problem to solve

• question to answer

Corrections by Hand

If you are writing your essay by hand, make any changes neatly. Use a caret (^) to indicate where you are inserting text.

Activity 1A Applying the Tips

Below is an essay written in response to the prompt, "Do the benefits of zoos outweigh the drawbacks?" Write changes in the margin next to each underlined word or phrase. At the end of the change, write the number of the tip that addresses this type of mistake.

Do you want to help save the Eastern Elk, one of the <u>big</u> animals found by the European settlers in North America? <u>You are too</u> late. <u>According the</u> Fish and Wildlife Service, this animal went extinct by the end of the nineteenth century. However, it is not too late for other animals. <u>I like zoos.</u>

One benefit of zoos is that they provide home for <u>species, that are becoming rare.</u> According to an article in *Scientific American,* "dozens of zoos across North America" work together to save endangered species, and they <u>have have</u> "helped bring black-footed ferrets, California condors, red wolves, and several other endangered species back from the brink of extinction."

In addition to providing shelter for endangered species, zoos can educate <u>poeple</u> about why we should protect animals. Research funded by the National Science Foundation found that "visitors believe they experience a stronger connection to nature as a result of their visit" to a zoo or an aquarium. <u>My brother worked at a zoo, and he really liked it.</u>

Critics say that zoos are terrible places for animals. <u>This is nutty.</u> However, modern zoos can offer large spaces and natural habitats for the animals in them. <u>Nevertheless,</u> living in the wild can be really terrible. Getting eaten by another animal is a horrible death.

Zoos, by saving species and <u>to make educated the</u> people, can help protect animals for the future Making zoos good places for animals might cost a little more money, but animals are worth it. For all <u>its</u> benefits, zoos deserve our support.

LESSON 2 GENERAL TEST-TAKING TIPS

Each chapter in this book offers tips and strategies that will help you in all writing that you do. The following five tips are particularly useful for writing well on a test.

☐ 1. Before the test, if you feel nervous, prepare yourself to concentrate. Close your eyes or focus on something that is not distracting. Take several slow, deep breaths. Remind yourself to relax.

☐ 2. Begin the test by quickly previewing all the prompts. This will tell what the test is about and how many texts you will write.

Finish Writing Before You Edit

Plan to save time to revise your writing. However, don't stop writing to revise. Finishing all tasks is more important than revising any single one.

☐ 3. Read each prompt carefully. Locate key words or phrases that will help you find the subject of the assignment.

☐ 4. Plan your time for each task. Allow a few minutes at the beginning of each task for prewriting and a few minutes at the end for revising. Use most of the time for writing.

☐ 5. As you begin to respond to each prompt, organize your thoughts about the topic. Use graphic organizers or outlines if they help you get your thoughts down quickly. Then begin writing.

Activity 2A Summarizing the General Tips

Summarize each of the five tips listed above into single words or short phrases.

1. _____

2. _____

3. _____

4. _____

5. _____

Activity 2B Writing About a Test

Write a short narrative about a student writing an essay on a test.
Include the five words or phrases you wrote in the previous activity.
Circle these words or phrases.

_____

_____

_____

_____

_____

_____

_____

_____

_____

_____

_____

_____

_____

_____

_____

_____

_____

_____

_____

_____

_____

Memory Devices

Connecting the test-taking tips in a story makes them easier to remember. Similarly, which set of words do you think is easier to remember?

- tests year school start students take often to the

- students often take tests to start the school year

The words are the same in both sets. However, since those in the second set are presented in the order of a single sentence, they are easier to remember. If you want to remember a set of key words, combine them into a sentence or short story.

LESSON 3 TIPS FOR SPEAKING AND LISTENING

Like reading, listening is a way to gather information. Like writing, speaking is a way to share what you know and think. The following list of tips will help you speak and listen effectively.

☐ 1. Prepare for a discussion by planning what you want to say. Know the evidence you want to refer to that supports your point.

☐ 2. Follow the rules of the discussion. Understand how often you should speak and how long you can speak.

☐ 3. Ask specific questions of other individuals in the discussion. Answer questions asked of you.

☐ 4. Review key ideas. Reflect on what they mean and practice paraphrasing them.

☐ 5. Identify a speaker's claims. Distinguish those that are supported by reasons and evidence and those that are not.

☐ 6. Interpret any images, graphics, or music that a speaker uses.

☐ 7. When presenting your idea orally, use appropriate eye contact, adequate volume, and clear pronunciation.

☐ 8. Use multimedia components, such as graphics, images, music, and sound, in your presentation.

☐ 9. Adapt your presentation to the context and the task.

> **Evaluating Speaking and Listening Skills**
>
> To become more familiar with the tips presented on this page, apply them to discussions held by others. Listen to a panel discussion on a television show. Evaluate how well the participants followed the tips.

Activity 3A Engaging in Discussion

Participate in a small group discussion about a topic about which you have or can gather much solid information. When your group is done, answer these questions about your discussion.

1. How well did members of the group refer to evidence on the topic?

_____

2. How polite were members of the group toward each other?

_____

3. How well did members of the group ask and respond to specific questions raised in the discussion?

_____

Activity 3B Interpreting Speeches

Take notes as you listen to a video of a speech or lecture on the Internet that presents an argument. Then answer the following questions about what you heard.

1. What was the speaker's argument? Identify the specific claims made by the speaker.

   _____

   _____

   _____

2. What reasons and evidence did the speaker provide to support his or her claims?

   _____

   _____

   _____

   _____

3. Explain whether you think the reasons and evidence supported the specific claims strongly or not.

   _____

   _____

   _____

   _____

Activity 3C Practicing a Speech

Have a friend videotape you as you present a one-minute excerpt from a famous speech. Review the videotape together and evaluate your speech on these issues:

1. Did you use appropriate eye contact?

   _____

2. Did you speak loudly enough to be heard easily?

   _____

3. Was your pronunciation clear?

   _____

Acknowledgments

Text Credits

"Year-Round School Improves Retention," by Mitchell Feldman. *Douglas Courier.* Marjory Stoneman Douglas High School. November 10, 2011.

"Defending the Traditional Schedule," by Boyd F. Jensen. *Deseret News.* January 30, 2011.

"Student Wins in J. S. v. Blue Mountain School District." From "Court Rules for Students in Pennsylvania Speech Cases," by Dave Warner. Reuters. June 14, 2011.

"Schools Confront Cyberbullying." From "Free Speech, Social Media Collide at Goodyear School," by Eddi Trevizo. Azcentral.com. April 30, 2012.

"The Other Wife," from *The Other Woman* by Colette.

Photo Credits

All photos are from Photos.com.